I Found the Answer
I Prayed

Josephine Fitzgerald

Copyright © 1996 by Josephine Fitzgerald

All rights reserved.

ROYALTY PUBLISHING COMPANY
P.O. Box 2016
Manassas, VA 20108

First Edition, December 1996

Printed in the United States of America

Library of Congress Catalog Number: 96-71921

ISBN 0-910487-40-5

DEDICATION

This book is dedicated to
a precious friend of mine, Betty Dunnevant,
who through much suffering has walked
humbly with her Lord.

Other books by Josephine Fitzgerald
When Thou Passeth Through the Waters
Precious Memories

TABLE OF CONTENTS

DEDICATION .... inside cover
ACKNOWLEDGMENTS ii
PREFACE iii
I FOUND THE ANSWER-I LEARNED TO PRAY iv

CHAPTERS   PAGES

1. Lord, Make Me Your Reservoir 1
2. The Reality Of Christ 12
3. What The Lord Orders—The Lord Pays For 21
4. Putting Feet To Our Prayers 29
5. ??God Speaks To Us?? 33
6. Our Lord Longs To Comfort 44
7. The Promise Box 54
8. God Wants To Deal With Love 62
9. How Israel Came Into Being 73
10. In The Midst Of Trials There Are Those
    Oasis In The Desert 81
11. Changing A Burden To A Song 84
12. God Never Makes A Mistake 91
13. Satan Cannot Get Into The Heart
    Of A Grateful Christian 95
14. Our God Is Sovereign 102
15. If You Are God's Child It Does
    Make a Difference 111
16. What God Was Able To Do Through
    One Woman That Was Open To His Word 116
17. A Burden For Souls 124
18. God Loves A Cheerful Giver;
    If We Give, He Will Give 129
19. A Life Fully Committed To The Lord 137
20. The Lord Is No Man's Debtor 152
21. Let's Let Our Light Shine 155
BIBLIOGRAPHY 158

ACKNOWLEDGMENTS

Thank you, Dolph Bell, Bob Campbell and Randy Bixler, for so graciously agreeing to read over this manuscript and making corrections and suggestions. I count you as special friends.

Thank you, Dr. Henry, Sue and Mona for going over the manuscript, making the final corrections and putting it on the computer, making it ready for the printer. They say if you want something done, go to a busy man. How true that is. I know of no one who is busier than you are, Dr. Jim Henry!

PREFACE

The Lord amazes me more and more. Each time He has wanted me to write another book, He has brought to mind some chorus I haven't heard for many years. The music goes over and over in my mind until I realize He is trying to get my attention. The hymn He gave me this time is *"I Found the Answer—I learned to Pray."* This beautiful hymn has such a wonderful message that I have reprinted it on the next page.

Again I have testimonies of others in this book; each testimony is an answer to someone's prayers. I hope this book will draw many people to a deeper prayer life with our Lord.

So many people feel like they don't know how to pray. It is so simple! As we feel a need, we turn to our Heavenly Father and tell Him all that is bothering us and ask Him to work it out for us. As we grow in Him, we begin to take others to Him, also. One thing is sure; we cannot have a real prayer life unless we stay in His Word. Bible study and talking to our Lord go hand in hand. We talk to Him, and as we stay in the Word, He answers us; otherwise, prayer would be one-sided. The more we know our Lord, the more confident we are that He answers our prayers.

Josephine

I FOUND THE ANSWER—I LEARNED TO PRAY!

I was weak and weary. I had gone astray.
Walking in the darkness, I couldn't find my way;
Then a light came shining to lead me from despair.
All my sins forgiven and I was free from care.

I found the answer—I learned to pray!
With faith to guide me, I found the way;
The sun is shining for me each day,
I found the answer—I learned to pray.

I was sad and lonely, all my hopes were gone,
Days were long and dreary, I couldn't carry on;
Then I found the courage to keep my head up high,
Once again I'm happy and here's the reason why:

I found the answer—I learned to pray!
With faith to guide me, I found the way;
The sun is shining for me each day,
I found the answer—I learned to pray.

Keep your Bible with you, read it every day.
Always count your blessings and always stop to pray;
Learn to keep believing and faith will see you through,
Seek to know contentment and it will come to you.

I found the answer—I learned to pray!
With faith to guide me, I found the way;
The sun is shining for me each day,
I found the answer—I learned to pray.

CHAPTER ONE

LORD, MAKE ME YOUR RESERVOIR

"Behold, I do a new thing: now it shall spring forth: shall ye not know it? I will even make a way in the wilderness, and rivers in the desert." (Isaiah 43:19)

As we grow in our Lord and seem to think we have our lives together, He often places us in an entirely new set of circumstances, and it seems as though we are starting our Christian life over.

There has been so much happening in my life since the last book, it is hard to know where to start. Two years ago, I had a heart attack and at the same time found I had diabetes. My life had to change drastically. Two months later, my son in Atlanta also had an heart attack, and several of the children and I went to see him. While there, the children expressed concern about my living alone. The Lord had been talking to me about that, so I asked Him to have the children approach me about it. My daughter told me what they had been discussing, and she added this. "Mama, I told them that I was your only daughter, so you are to come to live with me."

So we began to make plans. She was to see about a larger house and I was to sell my place in the Blue Ridge Mountains of Virginia and move down to Alabama the following winter. As I had given the house to the Lord, I didn't put it on the market, but let it be known by word of mouth that I was interested in selling my place—always taking it to the Lord that He wouldn't let me make a mistake.

I began having yard sales and took in over $1400 that I used to help publish my second book. As the things began to sell, several people came to look at the house, but various things stood in the way of their purchase plans. One day a buyer came; he was really excited. He was from out of town and had gotten a job where I live. The man wanted to bring his wife up to see the house. I really prayed that night that the Lord would not let me make a mistake.

The next morning when I went to the kitchen to fix breakfast, I had no water. I thought the spring needed cleaning. So when the people came, I explained that from time to time we had to clean the leaves and sand that gathered there. The prospective buyers told me that they wanted a couple of days to think it over and to pray about it. So we left it at that.

The next morning when I got up—out of habit—I turned the spigot on. The water came on full force. The Lord finally got through to me that I was not to sell my home. Later when my son came down, I sent him up to the spring to see if my neighbor had looked at and cleaned the holding box for me. In the past he had done that. When my son came back, he told me there was no sign that anyone had been there. I told him I had known all along that the Lord had sent His angels to take care of it.

When the man returned, he said due to his new job he decided to rent. I told him I already knew his answer because the Lord had given it to me. So I proceeded to tell him what happened. One thing is sure: if we really want to know the will of the Lord and are willing to obey Him, He will not let us make a mistake.

The Christmas holiday season is an extremely busy time for me—especially the first three weeks. Beginning at Thanksgiving, I have all the family that can come for dinner. I have the tree up, and we have Thanksgiving and Christmas sort of combined. Then, in the early part of December, I always have a Christmas party for my friends. Many of them are ministers and their families; so the party has to be early so as not to conflict with church schedules. From year to year, the number of people attending has increased. The last two years I had to divide and now, I have two parties a year. The day after the last party, two of my sons came down and packed me up to move. One of them took me to Notasulga, Alabama, to my daughter's home. Right after I left, the weather really started. They say that it was the worst winter we had in many a year. I had planned to stay two months, but as the winter weather continued, my other son wouldn't come to get me. I was there for four and a half months.

While I was in Notasulga, the Lord gave me a lovely illustration of our Christian life. I began to think of our water system. I live in the mountains. Way up on the mountains are two springs that have been diverted to run into a holding box. From there, they run into a 900-gallon reservoir, and from there to the house. We do not need a pump as the water has plenty of pressure. When leaves and sand build up in the holding box, the flow of water is affected. We have to clean it out periodically for the water to flow. When all is right, the water is continually flowing.

Our Lord has told us when we are full of the Holy Spirit—that out of our inner most being will flow rivers of living waters. We need to examine ourselves regularly as well as our springs. We need to be careful about all the little things that many times we let build up in us. So often we are guilty of gossip, lying, judging, etc. Also, we get away from reading the Word and praying. It clogs the channel that is between us and the Lord. We need to let the Holy Spirit sweep over us and bring to light the many things that have cluttered up our lives.

Once the clutter is clear, the overflow will come, and the Lord can reach many people through us. Even when we are not aware of it. <u>It is not us doing the work, but He is working through us</u>. Without Him, we are helpless. Yielded to Him, He draws the people to Him. As this unfolded to me, I was so excited and anxious to tell others about it. It's the little things that spoil the vine.

The next day after this was revealed to me, I was asked to bring a message to a church club. I knew immediately what I would speak on. When our Lord gives us insights, we need to pass them on. We can take in so much, and if we don't give it out, we get spiritual indigestion. And our ears get dull of hearing.

I have read somewhere that all of us have whole tracts of stubbornness. When we think we are fully yielded to Him, we are amazed at how we react when faced with new circumstances.

Since my husband died, I have opened my home to many of my loved ones with difficulties until they were ready to be on their own again. I have been blessed in seeing several of them come to a closer walk in the Lord. And I am sure others will respond in time.

Each time a new family or person comes, there is a lot of adjustment to be made by everyone. No two people do things alike. This experience has shown me how set I get in my ways. As we follow the Lord, we need to learn to be flexible, so the Lord brings all kinds of people into our lives. I am going to relate here several of the times when I reacted to things that made me wonder how I as a Christian could have reacted like that.

Once when one of my sons was living with me, I realized that something was really wrong, but I couldn't put my finger on it. I knew there was something between me and the Lord. I would pray and ask the Lord to reveal the problem. The phone rang, and my granddaughter answered it. When she hung up, I asked her who it was, and she told me it was her daddy. I asked her what he wanted. He told her not to tell me, she said. With that, I flew out the door, slamming it behind me. I plopped into the front porch swing, and all of a sudden the Lord opened my eyes, and I realized I had let a lot of resentment build up in my heart against my son. What a relief to lift my heart up to the Lord and have my peace restored. That afternoon when my pastor came over, I told him I had finally realized what had stopped my growth in the Lord. He was so glad that I had pinpointed it. He knew all along, but kept it to himself, praying the Lord would show me. Even if someone had told me, I wouldn't have believed it. I had to find out for myself. Surely, I thought as a Christian that I had gotten beyond that. The verse comes to me, **"Wherefore let him that thinketh he standeth take heed lest he fall"** (I **Corinthians 10:12**).

Another time, when I had several people living with me, something came up they all thought I needed to do something about. I felt the Lord was telling me to let Him work it out. One of them had been through a similar crisis and had failed to act, and it resulted in tragedy. The other had come across many cases like it in his line of work. Yet, the thought kept coming to me to just turn it over to the Lord. As they kept after me, one morning I decided to go with one of them and at least talk to someone. We started out and I asked the Lord to keep me from making a mistake. As we started out, my companion said he had some business to take care of first. The day passed, and we never got to the place they wanted me to go. That night the Lord spoke to me and said, *"You were ready to take the advice of one who is my child, but has drifted far away from me, and another who claims there is no God— rather than listen to me."* While we can listen to people, we must get our final answer from the Lord. If we really want His will, and ask Him not to let us make a mistake, He will guide us.

Dr. J. Gordon Henry sent me a prayer diary. In it is a quick checklist we were to go over before praying:

Are all sins confessed?
(Isaiah 59:1-2) (I John 1:9)
Are all relationships with others made right?
(Matthew 5:23, 24; Matthew 6:14, 15)
Are you seeking His will in all things?
(I John 5:14, 15)
Are you seeking to glorify God above all things?
(John 14:13, 14)
Are you depending on the Holy Spirit's guidance?
(Romans 8:26, 27)
Are you trusting God in spite of what seems to be?
(Proverbs 3:5, 6)
Will you praise God no matter what?
(Romans 8:28) (Thessalonians 5:16-18)

As I went over this checklist each day, I seemed to be stuck on the second one about relationships with others. I wasn't aware of any problems in this area, but I began to pray that God would reveal if anyone had anything against me or I had anything against anyone so we could get it straightened out. Be prepared to face many things when you pray that prayer!

The month before I had my heart attack was a difficult time for me. I was having many problems with my health. Something happened to my water. We had checked the reservoir, and the water was flowing freely. Even the overflow was overflowing. But no water was coming to the house. Many years ago, we had helped neighbors with their well and they never forgot it. They are always doing something for me, so when they heard about my problem they were right there to help me. My neighbor and his son decided the only way to find the trouble was to dig up the line. They both took the afternoon off and came down to find the trouble. I prayed that the Lord would lead them to the problem without so much trouble. That afternoon when they came over, his son was walking the water line. He was standing under the tree in my back yard. As he stood there, he started kicking at the leaves. A great stream of water came up. A root had rubbed a large hole in the pipe. My neighbor came to the door and knocked. When I got to the door, he was elated.

"The man upstairs must have been looking out for us," he said. We were so excited. We hugged each other and praised the Lord. While there was no open enmity between us, there had been a wall. When we were around each other, there was an uneasiness in both of us. Praise the Lord, whatever the problem, the Lord was answering my prayer!

Now I began to see why the Lord was opening the way for me to go to Alabama. While there, we went to quite a few places, and I was able to get many things worked out. We don't realize how a thoughtless word can wound another. I had never intentionally hurt anyone. We also forget to relay how much we appreciate what others have done for us. We praise the Lord, and many times forget to show our gratitude to others. Oh, the joy of having a bond of love between us again. I came back so refreshed. I am praying that I will be more thoughtful from now on. Much was accomplished in the four and a half months I was at my daughter's home. They were lovely to me, taking me on trips I needed to go on. There was much adjustment to be made there, and they did all they could and then some to make me comfortable. I could not have asked for better treatment. I am sure they were glad to relax when I left.

While there, I had a church away from home. Apart from Ridgecrest Baptist Church, here in Lovingston, Virginia, I would choose Salam-Macon Baptist Church in Notasulga, Alabama as my favorite church. The people are so friendly and love the Lord. The pastor's name is Bobby Carpenter. We had been without a pastor for over a year, and we had many people praying for us. I had been praying that the Lord would not let us get a pastor until we got the one that He had for us.

When my daughter Betty and I would go out, and people would ask the name of the pastor of her church, I would always say "Bobby Campbell," and Betty would correct me and say, "Mama, his name is Bobby Carpenter."

When I got home, the interim pastor was named Bobby Campbell. The Lord called him out of retirement, and now he is our pastor. Both of these pastors have wives who are real helpmates to their husbands.

****

****

CHARLOTTE CARPENTER'S TESTIMONY

I have always known that there was something very special about my husband, Bobby. From the time I met him in high school, I knew that he was different from anyone I had ever known. I always felt that God would definitely use my husband in service for Him, but I always felt that I would be his stumbling block. How could God ever use me?

The Lord began dealing with Bobby to answer the call to preach the gospel. At the time, we thought that God was asking us to leave our home-church of fifteen years to help out some smaller church that didn't have the talent and younger folks that we had at Line Creek. Little did we suspect that God had something totally different in mind.

We had struggled for sometime about what we were to do. God used a simple lesson my husband was trying to teach our daughter, Abbey, to show Bobby what He really wanted from him. He wanted Bobby to put his whole and complete trust in Him, just as Bobby wanted Abbey, blindfolded to take her daddy's hand and put her whole trust in him to lead her on a path she could not see.

Bobby came home from working the second shift one night. I noticed that he seemed to have something on his mind. As we sat at the kitchen table, he began to talk with me. He finally asked the question, "What would you say if I told you that God was calling me to preach?" I said, "It wouldn't surprise me in the least. I think I've known it for some time now." I don't know how to explain it, I only know that God told my heart before Bobby told my ears.

Again the question came to my lips, "I know God can use you, but how in the world will He be able to use me.?"

Since that time, God has answered that question over and over for me. He went before me. He used the years before He called us to mold me and bring me to the place where He could use me. While the ministry can be heartbreaking at times, it is the most rewarding and fulfilling life that I could ever have come to know. I thank God that He didn't look on the outside, but looked on the inside and saw what I could be when molded and made into His likeness.

TESTIMONY OF CALL INTO THE MINISTRY OF BOBBY CARPENTER

I was raised in a Christian home. My parents took me to church, and they lived the Christian life as an example for their children to follow. My father was a Baptist minister. Mom was devoted to loving her husband and raising her children to bring honor to the Savior. I was the only son among three daughters.

God drew me to Him, and I was saved when I was

about ten years old. Being a shy kid, I didn't like crowds very much. There was always this problem of low self-esteem. In high school I would not give oral reports. I didn't like talking in front of people, and I wouldn't if I could get out of it. I can honestly say that I never considered the thought that God might call me into the ministry one day. I knew God called men into His service. I knew my dad was called of God, but I didn't think I was the type that God could use in such a wonderful way.

When God began to lovingly turn me in His direction, I was already thirty-four years old. He had blessed me with a beautiful, multi-talented wife who loved me, a daughter who is a living testimony of the miracle working power of God, and He had allowed us to build our dream house. My wife and I had good jobs, and we were going to a great church with a dynamic pastor. I was a deacon and Sunday School teacher. My wife and I sang in the choir. Everything we had dreamed about and thought we wanted was given to us by the Lord.

Somewhere along the way things began to change. Family life was great. My church was wonderful, I loved my job, but my fellowship with God grew cold. I did all my church duties, but I knew that there was something dreadfully wrong in my relationship with God. It was a time of trying to pray to God, but only half-heartedly. Wanting to be led by the Lord, but wanting to go my own way, also. James said it best when he wrote, *"a double-minded man is unstable in all his ways."* **(James 1:8)** I wasn't in any spiritual condition to make any big decisions in my families' life.

Eventually, I lost interest in going to church. We didn't quit going as a family, but there just wasn't any joy anymore. It became more of a chore than a time of worship. It has always been a Baptist tradition to move your letter to another church if you become dissatisfied with where you are going, so I decided it was time for a change of scenery. The problem was, I loved my church. I loved the people there and the pastor. My wife and I had gone there for almost fifteen years. Leaving was going to be difficult. We did not want to go anywhere else. Where would we go?

Big decisions must be made and the leader of the family wasn't in any kind of spiritual condition to make the right choices. I began a search for God's will in my life. Books were purchased to help me make my decisions. Nothing was happening. My communication line with God was broken and I knew it. I was miserable.

I awoke one morning determined to try once more to ask God for guidance. By this time I was ready to be honest with myself and with God. I remember going into my daughter's bedroom and kneeling down to pray. Her room was special because I knew that there had been a time in my life when God had answered my prayers. You see, we couldn't have any children of our own and we asked God for a child. Within two months, God answered our prayers and gave us a daughter. It was there, in her room that I knelt and prayed, and for the first time that I can remember, I told the Lord that I would be willing to go or do anything He wanted me to. The answer came. It wasn't what I been expecting. There had been no forewarning, no inclinations as to what God had in store for me. God was calling me into the ministry. The one thing that I knew would never happen to me, just happened. But, I had prayed the prayer of complete obedience and God has given His answer. What could I do?

Not too long after this prayer of complete surrender I awoke one morning with the feeling that everything was going to work out. I hadn't told anyone what the Lord was wanting me to do, but I knew God was preparing me for what lay ahead. We had bought our daughter a new bicycle for Christmas, but it was too big for her to ride safely. I took the bike back to the store to exchange it. I brought home a new, smaller bike and put it under the carport at our house. My daughter wasn't home from school yet, and I wanted to surprise her. I didn't want her to see the bike before she got to the house. We had this long graveled driveway leading up to our house and every day after school I would walk down to the end of our drive and meet my daughter as she got off the school bus. On this particular day, I took a piece of cloth with me to blindfold her so she wouldn't see the bike too soon. She got off the bus. I explained to her about the surprise that awaited her up at the house, and I told her she had to wear the blindfold until we got to the surprise. She let me tie the cloth around her head to cover her eyes. I told her to take hold of my hand and I would lead her up the long graveled drive to our house. About half way up to the house I looked down and saw my daughter lifting up the blindfold with her free hand. She wanted to see where she was going. She wanted to see what was ahead. I told her to put both of her hands in mine so she would not be tempted to lift the blindfold. Up the driveway we went with her two hands in mine. Suddenly, I realized the Holy Spirit was speaking to me. Not in an audible voice, but in a voice just as clear. "Bobby, this is how I want to lead you. I want you to put both your hands in Mine. I don't want you to see where this new journey will take you. Partial obedience is not enough. Don't try to see where this new walk will take you. Put both of your hands in Mine, so you won't be afraid of where I will lead you." I knew that this was God. He had dialed my number. He gave me an opportunity to serve Him. He gave me the courage to accept His plan for my life.

After that encounter with the Lord, I began to see some changes God was making in me. He allowed me to fall in love with Him and His Word. He gave me a heart for souls, and a desire to reach out and help people. Most of all, God prepared my wife for what He was calling us to do. We sold our house and my wife worked to put me through Bible College. We left family and friends, and she never said a negative word. We are a team and God is our Leader.

God deals with everyone in different ways and manners. My calling was exactly what I needed to help me through the difficult times. The events and what happened in my life are important to me, but the greatest thrill is just to know that God is at work in my life.

CHAPTER TWO

THE REALITY OF CHRIST

"I am crucified with Christ: Nevertheless I live; yet not I, but Christ liveth in me; and the life I now live in the flesh by the faith of the Son of God, who loved me, and gave Himself for me." (Galatians 2:20)

I received a letter the other day that started me to thinking. The letter read, "Just a word to let you know I was thinking of you and thanking the Lord for the life you lived before us young women at Kingsland.

"The Lord has opened a ministry for my husband and me at a church for a season. My husband will be filling in until they get a full-time pastor. I know we will be sharing how we were saved, and I was thinking over how I came to receive Christ as my Savior. I can never think of that time without thinking of the short time at Kingsland and how the paths of our lives intersected. I do not recall any particular Bible truths from your class and teachings, but I do know I learned from your life. I can remember thinking that, 'This is a woman who knows God and He is real to her, not just stories on the pages of a book.' I think that was what Paul was saying in II Corinthians 3:2-3. Paul was an epistle before the Corinthians, and they were epistles of his effectiveness. As the saying goes, 'Our lives are the only Bible some people will ever read.'"

Then she adds, "Thank you for telling us about J. Vernon McGee and his *Through the Bible* program. I still listen and support him."

As I finished reading this letter my mind went back to that church and that particular class and that time in my life. Glad Billings had led me to the Lord about sixteen year earlier, and she always called us to come a little higher in our

Christian life. So I praise the Lord for bringing her into my life as we saw Christ in her. Because of the life that she lived, we wanted what she had. And as she fed us, we too wanted to make Christ real to others. She taught us that nothing was too small to take to our Lord, that He loved us and cared about everything that involved us.

In my classes, my greatest longing was to also make my Savior real to others. I realized that God had answered my prayer. Between Glad, her Bible studies and the church I attended the first fourteen years of my Christian life, I received a firm foundation in the Lord. So when the Lord called me to this church, I wanted all those dear ones to know the reality of our Lord. No matter what the lesson was about, I would make Christ the center of it, pointing out the importance of His work on the cross. Sometimes when I would go home, I would feel such a burden on me, that I would cry out to the Lord and ask Him to make me poured out wine and broken bread for the multitude.

The Lord took me at my word, and He is still working in my life. My one desire was to see my students turn their lives to the Savior in full surrender, that they too would want the Lord to fulfill the plan that He has for their lives. He gives us so many promises in His Word, and in many of them He stresses that *if* we but submit our lives to Him that He will do the work through us. As we stay in the Word and prayer, He does the work through us and we don't even realize it. That way, we can never take the glory. The glory belongs to Him and Him alone. In **Philippians 2:12-13,** He says, *"Therefore my beloved, as you have always obeyed, not as in my presence only, but how much more in my absence, work out your own salvation with fear and trembling; <u>for it is God that worketh in you</u> both to will and to do of His good pleasure."* And again we read in **Ephesians 2:8-10,** *"For by grace are ye saved through faith: and that not of yourselves: It is the gift of God: not of works lest any man should boast. For we are His workmanship, created in Christ Jesus unto good works, which God has before ordained that we should walk in them."* As I read these verses, I saw again God's plan for our lives. First, He went to the cross and paid for our sins, that we may have eternal life. As the Word says, "It is the gift of God." There is no way we can work for it. In **verse 10,** He makes it plain that He has created us into good works. For those of us who want our lives to count for Him, He has given us the Holy Spirit to enable us to live for Him. Our Lord never says that we have to live for Him, but He says, ***"If any man will follow me, let him deny himself, and take up his cross daily, and follow me" (Luke 9:23).***

A.J. Gordon wrote something I would like to share with you. *"We are wont to say that Christ died that we might not die. We should speak more truly if we affirmed that He died that we might die. He died for sin that we might die to sin: He bore our guilt in His own body that we might bear about His dying in our own bodies. Our wills surrendered to Christ, even as His will was surrendered to the Father's; our self-pleasing daily foregone for His sake,* **"who pleased not Himself;"** *our ease surrendered day by day in order that we may endure hardness as good soldiers of Jesus Christ, these are the crucial tests of discipleship. Our souls are saved only by Christ's outward cross of atonement; they are sanctified only by His inward cross of self-abnegation. . ."*

****

One day, I received this tract in the mail.
THE BROWN PAPER BAG
THE BRAG BAG

It was just an overstuffed ordinary brown grocery bag, but it held my heart's treasures. I kept it hidden in the far corner of my closet where no eyes but mine could see its contents.

God had anointed me to preach His Word. I have spoken in many places—churches, at Women's Aglow meetings, conventions, ladies' retreats and tent meetings. The Lord has given me great success in praying for the sick; hundreds have been healed. I also write for the ***Open Door Ministry,*** a world-wide tract ministry. I have received thousands of cards and letters of appreciation. The response has been great and letters of appreciation keep coming back to me. Over the years, I have kept those letters which had special meaning. These letters are the contents of my overstuffed ordinary brown paper bag.

In times of discouragement, I open the brown bag and encourage myself by reading the "nice things" said about me. They were reminders that my labors were not in vain. To me the brown paper bag was innocent and harmless—after all I did not flaunt its contents for others to see—but, as my birthday drew nearer this year I found my soul thirsting for the living God. I desired and asked the Lord for only ONE THING—that He would reveal Himself to me in such a way my emotions would be planted firmly on the Rock, Christ Jesus—so my body could be completely healed and new strength and a greater anointing could be on my life. Every time I prayed this way, I was reminded of the brown paper bag hidden in the corner of my closet.

Finally, the night before my birthday, I emptied the contents of the brown paper bag on the floor and inquired of the Lord if there was something there that He wanted? The Lord spoke to my heart. "This is your BRAG BAG. It continues your applause and *well done* of men. Can you give it ALL to Me?"

I did not fully understand what God was saying to me until I put ALL the contents of my BRAG BAG into a garbage bag for the trash collectors. When I became obedient, the Lord opened my eyes to these scriptures:

"You cannot please both God and man."
"Encourage yourself in the Lord."
(not in other people's opinions)
"Make your boast in the Lord."
(not in the brag bag)

Check your life and heart out with the Word of the Lord to see if you can be the "apple of His eye" (not the apple of the eyes of others).

THE LORD IS A JEALOUS GOD. He will have no other gods, idols or Issacs before Him. He shall have a people whose eyes are stayed on Him. Neither flattery nor spittle shall turn their heads.

Every Issac of our hearts must be put on the altar in this hour. What is not surrendered fully to the Lord will be shaken until our desire is for the Lord Jesus Christ—our Heavenly Bridegroom! As I walked my BRAG BAG out the back door to the trash cans, I held it before the Lord and declared with my whole heart, "EVERYTHING that these cards and letters represent I surrender to you. If there be any praise, if there be any honor or any glory—I give it all back to you, Lord!"

It was then I heard another *"Well done"* and I knew my emotions had found their place in the Lord, and God had, at last, His rightful place in my heart and affections. For this time the *"Well done"* was not the voice of a man, but the ONE from ABOVE!

by Eleanor Grace Armstrong

As I read this tract, the Lord spoke to my heart. While I had not had the type of ministry that she had, my Lord had led me into a ministry that He had for my life. For each of us He has a special plan. And the amazing thing is what He has for each of us. It is always something we would never dream of, at least it was with me.

He led me into writing books—I, who had not even had a high school education. I, too, received many letters, and as the tract writer, I have had a struggle with the letters.

The Lord spoke to me about it, and I couldn't believe that I had touched His glory. I confessed it to the Lord, but it seemed to creep back again! So after reading the tract, I, too, put all my letters into a trash bag and took them to the dumpster. You would think after that things would be fine. Satan never leaves us alone and now I am faced with the fact that before I destroy them, I generally let several people read them, so again I cry out to the Lord. The longing of my heart is that my precious Lord, and He alone, will get all the glory, honor and praise. I, too, long to hear His *"Well done, my good and faithful servant."*

I have learned (or hope I have) how much we need to guard our hearts every minute. Satan tries in every way to plant something there, and soon if we don't watch ourselves, we are thinking that way. <u>We can only live our lives for the Lord through the power of Holy Spirit.</u> Again, "<u>Without Him, I can do nothing.</u>"

REV. FREDERICK ZELLER'S TESTIMONY

I was saved on August 5, 1975 at a teen "rap" meeting in upstate New York. The meeting was held in a neighborhood home with a young future pastor leading. About twenty young people attended the meeting and this was the second meeting I had attended.

I was challenged on my relationship with God. I admitted that I had no relationship with Him, that I was a sinner, and that Jesus died for me. God gloriously saved me and started me on a path that changed my life. Instead of a broad road to Hell, I was on the narrow road to Heaven.

I was discipled by godly people for two years in a Bible believing Baptist church. The pastor and the people took it upon themselves to love me through several growth stages. I thank God for Christians who looked beyond what I was to what I could be.

In 1977, I graduated from high school and set off for a calling that I was not sure of. I knew I was to work for Christ and Him alone, but how and where? I enrolled in the Thomas Road Bible Institute in Lynchburg, Virginia. In two years, I finished my education and also met a special young lady, my future wife, Susan. She was a student at Liberty Baptist College (now Liberty University). We were married in December of 1979.

I later enrolled at the Institute of Biblical Studies at Liberty. Susan and I both graduated in the spring of 1981. We moved to Fredericksburg, Virginia and both went to work in a Christian school. I went to work for two years and then worked for two more years elsewhere in a secular vocation.

In May of 1984, God moved on my heart to fulfill a calling He gave me in 1980. I answered the call to preach at Leesville Road Baptist Church, outside of Lynchburg, one Sunday after much counsel with my pastor, Ron Lynch. I had not done much after that about the call. I answered the call by going back to college as a pastoral major. My course was set. In 1985, I would go to school and finish preparing for God's call.

If you have lived the Christian life for very long, you know that God has a way of confirming His call in your life. God had quite a way of doing that in my life. In September of 1984 I started to get sick. I had the flu, but it passed. I had strange feelings or lack of feeling in my trunk area. This will pass, I said, but it did not. It got so bad that within a couple of weeks I was in an ambulance. My blood pressure was dangerously high and I could not feel anything from the waist down. I was paralyzed in my legs.

The doctors told me that I had a rare disease that only a handful of people, nationwide, ever got during the year. That was not the end of it. This disease had a twenty per cent mortality rate and if I did live, I might not ever get completely well.

Wait a minute! Had I not answered the call? Had I not planned to do what God had called me to do? How could this be happening to me?

I do not remember saying any of these things. God gave me a peace, that to this day, I do not understand. I knew that He was in control and no matter what shape I was in, ministry was still possible.

After a month's stay in the hospital and five months of rigorous physical therapy, I could walk pretty well. I had to learn to walk all over again and learn what my limitations would be for the short and the long term.

In the fall of 1985, I was off to school with my wife and our new little girl, Margaret. (Oh, I forgot to mention that my wife was pregnant during my entire sickness.) I attended Appalachian Bible College in Beckley, West Virginia.

Upon finishing college, we returned to Fredericksburg and Susan and I again taught in a Christian school. I was also the Assistant Pastor of our church. It was a good time of using what I had learned and learning much more about church life and people.

In the winter of 1988, the church decided the new pastor did not need an assistant. I was relieved without warning in a business meeting. What would I do? Nothing. God did all the work. A businessman by the name of Don Garrett came to me and said he wanted me to work for him. (I mention Don's name for he is in need of a heart transplant today. Pray for him.) I worked for Don for five years in the electronics field. God had actually answered a prayer of mine by giving me this job. I had prayed that God would allow me to have a trade to use in the ministry if I would need to be bivocational.

In 1989, Susan and I moved into a new house. I was working full-time and God was blessing us. Within a short time, God led us to Ladysmith Baptist Church where Roger Gorby pastors. Roger is a man who loves Jesus and loves the souls that Jesus died for. He had a great part in my becoming a pastor.

I worked with the Sunday School and youth while at Ladysmith. Susan and I were making good friends and loved every part of that growing church. There were great possibilities for ministry in that community, but God had something else in mind for me.

Roger started working with me in getting a pastorate. In less than a year, Rockfish Valley Baptist Church called me to be their pastor. God was allowing me to shepherd a group of His people. That teenager who was saved from a life of sin, discipled by people who saw farther than what he looked like, and directed by Spirit-led people, was fulfilling God's call in his life.

My life verse is **Philippians 1:21**. *"For me to live is Christ and to die is gain."* This verse has been on my mind and in my heart since high school. I can do nothing *"for it is God which worketh in you both to will and to do of his good pleasure"* (**Philippians 2:13**).

SUSAN K. ZELLER'S TESTIMONY

The past gives evidence of God's goodness, power, and His life-giving love. Not until I thought back on the events before and during my husband's illness could I clearly see how God blessed our lives. Things such as protecting Fred as he drove only days before he lost all muscle control. Renewing an insurance policy that kept us from becoming financially disabled. Allowing me to conceive only two months before the illness after five years of marriage.

Fred was experiencing a life change directly from the hand of God and I have reaped benefits from that. The first Sunday back to church after a month in the hospital, we sang a hymn that has become precious to me, "Great Is Thy Faithfulness." Because of His faithfulness my spirit was renewed and got me through the long days of watching Fred progress from a wheelchair, to a walker, to a cane. The doctors never knew when or if the healing would continue. Attitudes of anxiety would many times turn to disappointment. God in His graciousness does not allow us to see the future, just to walk with us through it.

It has taken me many years to accept some things that resulted from Fred's illness that cannot be changed, but I accept that they were for my good.

The greatest good came from having a husband that allowed God to change his heart. Everyone ultimately benefits from a heart that surrenders to the will of God.

CHAPTER THREE

WHAT THE LORD ORDERS— THE LORD PAYS FOR

"Now unto him that is able to do exceeding abundantly above all that we ask or think. According to the power that worketh in us.
(Ephesians 3:20)

When I first started writing, the Lord told me that the books were to be given out freely to those who could not afford to give a donation. He promised that He would lay it on people's hearts to send in enough to support the ministry. It was never meant as a money-making project. We have always had enough to pay the final payment whenever the books were at the printers. Mostly with nothing over, but the Lord always built up the account again.

I received a letter today that is a real challenge to our faith; (it should not be, as the Lord has never let us down). I will print the letter verbatim.

> Dear Josephine:
> By the time your receive this letter, your book will have all corrections and sending to Washington, to Margareti, where she will type the final Spanish version.
> I ask you to give this testimony in your church and ask them to pray a prayer for the financial need to print the book in Spanish. From that prayer meeting the Lord will bring someone who will be touched by the Spirit to do the work of the Lord.
> Correcting your book has brought the

Word to my life again. So this book will be a blessing and a need, a must in the Spanish world.

God bless you,
Aida

After reading that letter, my thoughts went back to the time when my son was going to the Beth Messiah Congregation right outside of Washington, D.C. While he is not Jewish, he loves the Jewish people. At this point in his life, he was living in Virginia Beach, and attending the Beth Messiah there.

The Lord had spoken to Aida in Venezuela and told her He had a job He wanted her to do in America. In obedience to her Lord she packed up and came to her sister's house in Virginia Beach. Although she isn't Jewish either, she also has a love for God's people. One Saturday she also attended the Beth Messiah, where she met my son. She told him that the Lord had sent her on a mission, but she wasn't sure at this point what it was. After services that day, the Lord spoke to her and told her that He wanted her to attend the Beth Messiah outside of Washington the next week. Aida asked the Lord to provide a way for her to get there. The following Friday, my son called her and told her that he was going to Washington to attend the Beth Messiah the following day. He asked her if she would like to go. He also told her that he would be coming to my home in Lovingston, Virginia, to spend the night and go back the following day. On the strength of what the Lord told her, she accepted the ride.

After the services were over that day, they came to my home. We had a lovely visit, and in the course of the conversation my son told her I had written a book. That night when I took her to her room, I gave her several books in case she wanted to read. My book was among them.

She attended my church with me the following day. After church, when we came home, I had several guests for lunch. As I was preparing the meal, Aida stayed on the front porch. I asked her if she wanted to come in. She told me that she loved it out there. Looking at the mountains made her feel close to the Lord. When lunch was ready, Aida came in and filled her plate and went back on the porch. My granddaughter, Nicole, was here to spend some time with my son, her daddy. I noticed that when she filled her plate, she also went outside.

When the company left, Aida wanted to talk to me. So we found a private place, and she began to share with me what the Lord had spoken to her. The conversation went something like this: "The Lord spoke to me and said, 'I want you to talk to Nicole and encourage her.' I said, 'I don't even know her.'" At that point Aida said, the Lord gave her a vision of Nicole crying herself to sleep every night. After that she told the Lord if He would send Nicole to her she would do her best. Right after that she saw Nicole come out on the porch and she was able to comfort her.

Aida again shared with me that when she went to bed that night, as she picked up my book, the Lord spoke to her again and told her to be careful with that book because it was a holy book. He also told her that He wanted her to take the book back to Venezuela and translate it into Spanish. She then asked me for permission to do the translation. Of course, I gave it. She was in Virginia two more weeks, then went back home.

I didn't hear from her for about two years. Then one day, I received a letter. She told me that so much had happened that she hadn't had time to work on the book. However, she had led a young couple to the Lord. The wife was a translator.

When Margareti (the translator) heard about the book, she told Aida that she would love to translate it as a labor of love for her Lord. He had done so much for her.

Not very long after that, the Lord led Margareti and her family to move to America. They settled in northern Virginia. Margareti called me and told me that she had finished the translation and would put it on a computer as soon as she had access to one. Not long ago, she called me and told me she had sent it back to Aida. And now I have received this letter from Aida!

As I write this and am again reviewing it, I feel so

humble. To think that the Lord chose me out of so many people to do the writing as He led me to write. He distributed the books—an impossibility for me out in the country. I don't even drive! Then, He sent a girl all the way from Venezuela to speak to my granddaughter, and to lay on her heart to take the book to translate it into Spanish. Will wonders ever cease? I stand in awe of our Lord. **TRULY HE IS LORD OF LORDS AND KINGS OF KINGS. PRAISE HIS NAME.** May I always see things being brought about by Him and Him alone!

How can I ever doubt that the money will not come in after all He has done? It will be exciting to watch and see how He will work it out. **Oh, how exciting it is to be a Christian. We never know what He is going to do next.**

I often think of how the Lord led in Dr. Henry having a prayer seminar at my church. I signed on as a doorkeeper. So each month a Doorkeeper Report was mailed to me. My name was on the prayer calendar. I always look forward to that day when people would be praying for me. I could always feel the difference.

As I began writing, Dr. Henry always took the time to answer my letters. I always looked forward to those letters, as the Lord always had a message for me in them. Sometimes if there was something that I had been struggling with there would be a phrase or comment in the letter that made that thing a little clearer to me, although he had no idea at the time what I may have been going through. That is what happens when you allow the Holy Spirit to work through you. Dr. Henry is definitely a Spirit-filled man. He is a humble man and so anxious to tell everyone about the change that took place in his life in 1977. Dr. Henry has preached the gospel ever since he was a 17-year old boy, back in the mountains of Kentucky.

One day, he picked up a book written by George Mueller. As he read it, he realized that every time he was studying the Bible it was to prepare a message and then he would pray about his ministry and ask the Lord to bless it. He realized that he needed to take time to spend with the Lord solely for his own growth. Also he learned that prayer was to be the most important thing in his life. As he took time to study the Bible for his own soul, he was led to pray for others. As he continued his quiet time for his own soul, it began to change his life. The Lord led him to teach his people about this.

At this time he had been with Liberty Baptist College for six years, as vice-president for Academic Affairs and dean of the college. While there, the school grew from a few students to 1,800. The faculty had grown to over 100. He also pastored Pleasant View Baptist Church in Lynchburg, VA. As the Lord began to give him the vision of a deeper life with Him through prayer, he began to teach his people, and they too grew in the Lord. While he has updated his materials as the Lord revealed it to him, the basics that he learned then are what we receive in the prayer seminars that he holds around the world.

It really humbles me when I read about the thousands that the Lord has used him to minister unto, that he would take time out of his busy schedule to do the final editing of the books the Lord led me to write.

I was reading the following in my doorkeeper report and asked his permission to include it in the book. He graciously gave me permission.

ONE MILLION MILES
BY DR. J. GORDON HENRY

I don't regret a mile that I've traveled for the Lord! On Friday evening, January 27, 1995—driving from Phoenix to Flagstaff, Arizona—a milestone was achieved in the prayer seminar ministry. The one millionth mile was reached and surpassed! Certainly, this was a thrilling moment as well as a call to renewed commitment to the work the Lord has given to me.

I stand amazed in the call of God to conduct the prayer seminars and in His gracious provision and protection in traveling from place to place. For me, this has been a time of reflection.

The preparation
    My own metamorphous in my spiritual life came in 1977 when prayer and Bible reading (for my own food, rather than preparation for a sermon to preach) came into focus for me in a vibrant, refreshing, life-changing way. The outworking of new understanding was the prayer chapel ministry in Virginia—with someone praying in the chapel every hour around the clock. To prepare the 168 plus prayer warriors, weekly studies were prepared and taught during the church training hour Sunday nights. These eight studies have become sessions of the ***Prayer Seminar Workbook***. Although I have revised and sharpened a number of the sections as the Lord has given me additional insight, the basic material is what was written in 1977.
    The next step in the preparation came in 1980 when, after over 1400 Sundays serving as a local church pastor, an invitation came to assume the presidency of Northeastern Bible College (NJ) in the New York City area. My weekends were available to share with churches. My initial dream was to develop a prayer chapel ministry involving administrators, faculty, and students on the campus. My intention was to raise funds for a chapel in memory of my best friend, Hugh Bryan Mylam, who had gone home to be with the Lord in May 1980 at the age of eighty-five. The reaction was quite negative. I was reminded that funds needed to be raised—operating funds and deficit reduction funds. God had another plan.
    Upon learning about the prayer chapel ministry in Virginia, our pastor at Madison Baptist Church asked if I would lead a prayer emphasis sharing all I had learned about prayer. My response was, "Sure, I already have the material written"—the sessions prepared for the prayer warriors in Virginia which were typed on stencils and mimeographed. At the same time, the Christian radio station in South Orange invited me to lead thirty-minute programs Monday through Saturday during the month of August. My theme was prayer and the response was amazing as listeners called the station wanting to talk with me. During the programs, I referred to the prayer "seminar" at Madison Baptist Church scheduled for October 5-8, 1980. Soon other churches wanted to

schedule seminars. It wasn't long until Sue and I were traveling somewhere every weekend—usually to conduct a prayer seminar.

The seed planted

An invitation came to serve as the keynote speaker for the annual missionary conference at Sunbury Bible Church, Sunbury, Pennsylvania. My assignment was to kick off the conference with two messages on Sunday, March 20, 1983 and return for the final session on Wednesday night, March 23, which would feature a singing group from Northeastern Bible College. On Sunday, the Lord moved mightily in a discernible, clear way. Although I usually extended a public invitation for decisions at the end of my message, I followed the tradition of many churches in the North and did not.

The church asked that we come early to enable a time of interaction between the college students and the senior high group. While the youth were meeting, I was invited to share a meal with the missionary speakers. As soon as I sat down, several missionaries began to share the impact of the Sunday services. One said, "All the people talked about all the week were the Sunday services." Another one remarked, "If you had given an invitation Sunday, several hundred would have come forward."

Again, the Holy Spirit moved mightily. When I finished the message, I extended a public invitation and several hundred responded! I stood on the platform and Pastor Roland Gerdes was down on the floor with the people who had responded. He looked up to me and said, "When can you schedule a prayer seminar for us?" My answer was it would be a long time because I tried to give priority to the work of the college working until 5 p.m. on Friday and back in the office at 8 a.m. on Monday. His response planted the seed: "Why don't you let the college get another president and you get out on the road. You have something special to share!"

I had never thought of such an idea. You will remember that for twenty-seven years I was a pastor who preached twice on Sunday and led a mid-week service. Although I had an extended ministry through leading revival meetings in other churches, my base was fixed.

Although the students shared their excitement about the meeting as we drove back to Essex Fells, I can't say I heard a word they were saying. The car wheels seemed to cry out, "On the road. On the road. On the road."

The move

Things moved rather rapidly. Dr. John Hash, Bible Pathway Ministries, Murfreesboro, TN, invited me to set up offices with him and conduct the prayer seminars out of Bible Pathway. In late July 1983, we moved to 2319 Floyd Drive, Murfreesboro, a property which had a back lot at 2114 Arrow Court.

The Transnational Association of Christian Colleges and Schools (TRACS) invited me to become their executive director which provided an opportunity to continue to work in higher education while conducting the prayer seminars. In May 1984, J. Gordon Henry Ministries became a reality when we were incorporated in the State of Tennessee. Offices were established on the square in Murfreesboro at 210 West Main Street. In September 1987—through the help of partners in the prayer seminar ministry—we moved into our own building at 2114 Arrow Court, the lot at the back of our house.

There have now been 620 prayer seminars in forty-two states, the District of Columbia, and twenty-four nations.

No regrets

I don't regret a mile I have traveled for the Lord. Beyond that, I am ready to continue on the journey knowing the Lord has called and that He has given us partners known as **Doorkeepers** who are very much a part of what we are doing. Don't forget to remember to pause at this time to *"praise the Lord who daily loads us with benefits"* (**Psalm 68:19**).

CHAPTER FOUR

PUTTING FEET TO OUR PRAYERS

"Pure religion and undefiled before God and the Father is this, to visit the fatherless and widows in their affliction, and to keep himself unspotted from the world." (James 1:27)

The Lord leads us into many ministries as we walk with Him. For several years, He gave me the joy of ministering in several nursing homes. As I went to visit these people, I felt like they became part of my family. When something happened to them, I also felt the pain.

One day when I was on visitation, I met a friend. She introduced me to the activity director, Pat Mendoza. As we talked, my friend mentioned to Pat that I had written a book. So I gave Pat a copy. After reading the book, she asked me to come and have a Bible class for the patients. As we met in one of the patient's rooms, she would bring three or four others. Afterward I would go in various rooms and read the scripture and pray.

Our church started to have services at the nursing home one Sunday a month. I was able to meet quite a few more of the patients and so my "family" grew. It was hard to watch them deteriorate from day to day. I loved them so much. I am thinking of several I have visited—some still living, others have gone on.

Hallie is a very special friend; she has a deep faith that cannot be shaken. She is blind, but she can see forms. She has one leg and bursitis. When I visited Hallie, Catherine, another friend, would sing and I would read scripture. We would all pray. Hallie knew that we lived alone and would caution us to be careful. Once a friend of mine whose son was a minister was visiting Hallie. It was a hot sunny day so this friend had worn shorts. Hallie put her hand on her knee, and in a very sweet way, told her that if she wore shorts, she could hinder her son's ministry. My friend never wore them again. We knew that Hallie loved us so we were not offended when she scolded us. Hallie is one of the fortunate ones as her family visits her regularly.

Hallie's roommate is my dear friend, Myrtle. Before Myrtle had to go to a nursing home, she came to see me most every day. Myrtle was a hard person to talk to and I would ask the Lord to show me how to draw her out. It was around Christmas when she started coming regularly, so the Lord led me to pick up a hymnbook. I would start singing the old Christmas carols. At first she just listened, then I would hear her join in. As we sang, her voice got stronger. Then we would have lunch together. We sang *"The Old Rugged Cross"* often. She said, "I sing it so much someone ought to sing it at my funeral." Her mind began to go, and as she needed 24 hour-a-day care, they put her in a nursing home. She doesn't recognize visitors, but talks all the time. It breaks my heart to see her in that condition.

Across the hall, there was a man who talked about the Lord all the time. He came to my Bible class. One day, I took my New King James Version of the Bible and as I was reading, he stopped me and told me, "That won't no Bible." I had to get the King James Version before we could continue. He loved to go to other people's rooms and talk to them about the Lord. As his mind was going, he was moved away. Later, I heard that he died.

Next to his room was a lovely couple, Ressie and Abe. She was always smiling and always helping someone. Abe is precious, but he stays closer to his room. We often talked about how dependent he was on her and wondered what he would do if anything happened to her. She seemed so young that we never dreamed anything would happen. But, she got sick and had to go to the hospital. It wasn't long before she died. Now, Abe is pitiful. He sits in his chair most of the time. When we go there and talk to him about the Lord, he shakes his head and says, "He's the onliest one." Abe can't read or write, so whenever I can go see him I always try to read to him. He has no children, but his nieces and nephews visit him.

The man now in Abe's room doesn't talk to him at all. (I don't think he can talk.) When anyone talks to him, he just stares and looks like a defiant little boy. I always go over to him and tell him that Jesus loves him. The only response I get is a frown. I will pat him and laugh. I think he would be disappointed if I failed to go speak to him.

One day I had a Bible study in one of the small rooms. We had finished and most of the people had gone when a man walked in and started a conversation. During the conversation, I asked him if he was a Christian. He said, "No." So I asked him if he would like to be saved, and again he said, "No." With that he left the room.

That Sunday a retired preacher, who was confined to a wheel chair gave a gospel message, and issued an altar call. The man didn't respond. That night he died. The Lord kept giving him opportunities to be saved, up to the last minute.

That precious man, a retired preacher, was placed there by the Lord, I firmly believe. He had never married, and his only relatives were two sisters who had never married either. As he was confined to a wheelchair, they had to put him where he could get the help he needed. As long as he was able, he went up and down the halls, trying to lead souls to the Lord. It was a big mission field. It was a sad day when he went to the hospital and didn't come back. His roommate never had visitors, so our church took him under our wings and we would visit him. He was hard to talk to, but we would go and assure him of the Lord's love. He only had one leg. He had a picture of three nice boys in Navy uniforms. As I knew that he had been in the service, I asked him which one was his picture. With tears in his eyes, he told me they were his sons. I had heard that he had neglected his family and that now they wouldn't have anything to do with him. What a price we pay when we walk in our own way! I do believe he is in heaven. I am sure that his roommate had a lot to do with that, as he lived Christ before him day by day.

There are three others I will write about. Frances came

from North Carolina. When she became sick, her husband took her to the hospital to find out what was wrong. The test revealed palsy. While seeking the right medication, she was given a medicine that caused her feet to turn inward. She is now in a wheelchair. After her husband's death, her children brought her to a nursing home in Virginia where they could visit her regularly. I found myself spending more and more time with her. She has given her heart to the Lord.

Pat Mendoza left and Joyce Quick became the activity director. One day Joyce called me and asked me if I would take the month of November to have Bible classes once a week. I agreed; she set it up in a large dining room. That was in 1993. The lessons were all about how much the Lord loved them and ended with how He gave His life for them. My friend Catherine agreed to take me, and also to lead the singing. The people loved to hear her sing. I will always be grateful for that time, as it turned out to be the last time I got to minister to them regularly. Our Lord's presence was there. Two weeks later I was on my way to Alabama.

Now for the other two. One little black lady stayed in her room. When I would go to invite her to join Bible study, I would feel I was on holy ground. Her Bible would be open before her. Her face was aglow—you knew that she had been with Jesus.

The other lady is also black. She is 102 years old. As you approach her, she smiles and puts out her fist like she wants to box. She is always talking about her heavenly home. She told me when I got there she would be in the choir waiting for me.

Catherine's mother was in a home. It was through initial visits to her that we met these people which led to wonderful opportunities to minister. That also led Catherine and me to start visiting in different nursing homes as a team. That was truly a blessed experience. The memories will last for a lifetime!

CHAPTER FIVE

??GOD SPEAKS TO US??

> *"How shall they call on him in whom they have not believed? And how shall they believe in him of whom they have not heard? And how shall they hear without a preacher? And how shall they preach except they be sent/ As it is written, how lovely are the feet of them that preach the gospel of peace, and bring good tidings of good things! Faith cometh by hearing; and hearing by the word of God."* (Romans 10:14, 15, 17.)

GOD SPEAKS TO US THOUGH THE PREACHING OF THE WORD

Many times I would start to church with a real problem on my mind, and I would be praying and asking the Lord to reveal to me the answer. On two occasions when I got to church the preacher would say, "You folks pray for me: the Lord won't let me preach the message I prepared, but has said I am to preach on this subject. That sermon would answer my question in detail. I knew it was the Lord speaking to me. If we really want to know His will He will tax heaven if necessary to see that we have His answer. One time in particular, when I was studying about the tabernacle, there was one point I couldn't seem to understand. That morning the pastor had a blackboard on the platform and described in detail what I needed to know even though he could see no reason for it, he obeyed the voice of the Lord.

One day I was asked to give my testimony in my Sunday school class. As I spoke, I looked up and the pastor was standing in the door listening. The Lord revealed to him why he was asked to do that.

Where the gospel is preached in the power of the Holy Spirit, lives are touched and transformed. Some for the first time hear the gospel and are saved. Others that are saved have the word opened to them in a fresh way and are eager to learn more. I feel this is the highest calling of all.

Way before the Lord begins to speak to us, The Holy Spirit is laying ground work in our hearts. Along the way, people have sown seeds that have laid there and every once in a while someone else will water it. Then comes the time when they are ready, and by the preaching of the word, our Lord will bring the increase. Our Lord Jesus alone can save through the blood He shed at Calvary.

When one is saved, we need to disciple him until he is strong enough to go to the Word of God himself. We need to remember that he is a babe and needs the milk of the Word and that through us he is brought to the place that he is ready for the meat of the Word. If he is in a sound Bible-believing church, he is not apt to depart from the Word.

THE SECOND WAY THE LORD SPEAKS TO US IS
THROUGH TEACHERS, EITHER IN CHURCH OR
HOME BIBLE STUDIES

My own experience was through a home Bible class. My teacher was Spirit-filled. She always encouraged us to come a little higher, and as we studied under her, first we came to Jesus for salvation and went on to become mature Christians always yearning to come a little higher in our Christian walk. As in a home Bible class, we grew in a close knit group, and we encouraged each other along the way. Before I was a Christian, I used to think attending the eleven o'clock service was enough. After I was saved, I realized how important it was to attend all the services of the church. If we really want the Lord to be a living Lord in our lives, we must stay in the Word. In **Psalm 42:1-2** the psalmist says, *"As the hart panteth after the water brooks, so panteth my soul after thee O God, for the living God: When shall I come and appear before God?"*

Have you heard the story of the deer? In a certain country, once a year the deer hear the call for the water brooks. First they become restless. Then, they take off in a run to try to reach the place. Along the way the faint hearted and weak ones drop by the wayside, but the ones that are determined to get there will persevere. So it is with us. We who are determined to live for our Lord will keep on keeping on, even though at times we may fall. We will get up more determined than ever to yield our lives to the Lord. It is only in yielding that we grow. No matter what we do, if self is in the way, we are working in the energy of the flesh and it is not God working through us. The most important time of all is the quiet time we have with Him. not to study or prepare a sermon, but to just read His Word and talk to Him because we love Him. Then He can reveal His plans to us—not always—but when we are ready to hear them. We sit at His feet and tell Him all that is bothering us. We read His Word and allow Him to talk to us. It is not a time for us to tell Him how to work out the problem, but to just lay it at His feet.

GOD SPEAKS TO US IN SONGS

Last night my pastor and his brother, Don, gave us a good old gospel singing. They sang all the old hymns that have meant so much to me through the years. As they sang, it brought back memories. I could visualize each song and where I was when the Lord spoke to me, through them. Truly He has promised us songs in the night. Always when He is ready for me to start another book, a certain chorus will run through my mind until I realize what He wants me to do. Many times when I was discouraged, He would bring the right song to mind that would uplift me. When our hearts are open, He will give us songs in the night.

ANOTHER WAY HE SPEAKS TO US IS THROUGH THE WORD

I have had a heavy burden on my heart many times, and would be reading my Bible, when almost out of nowhere it seemed that a verse would lift itself out of the Bible and flash the words before my eyes, always it would be the answer to the question I had in mind. When the Lord gives you a verse it is always yours. We have many verses in the Bible that are promises, and I have heard people say, "Get hold of one of those verses and make it your own", and I am sure that is true. But how wonderful when the Lord brings the promise to you. It isn't a matter of claiming it. It is just accepting what the Lord has told you in His word. There is no way you can doubt it. When I get a new Bible I never feel it is mine until I underline each of these special verses and many times I write under them what I was going through at the time and claim the answer. Those verses are not isolated verses. They are your very own, given to you by the Lord. While He gives me new ones also, the Holy Spirit brings back to me these verses as I need them. When writing about this, the Scripture that comes to mind is *"Faith cometh by hearing; and hearing by the Word of God"* (**Romans 10:17**). I think that most of us hear the Word of God from preachers first. That is why the Lord calls out preachers and missionaries to go forth and tell the good news to others.

Where the gospel is preached in the power of the Holy Spirit, many souls are saved and many answer the call to a deeper walk with Him. I feel that is the highest calling of all.

The story was told about Robinson Crusoe and his man Friday. I don't remember it all, but he had gotten down and could not do for himself. He had Friday open an old sea chest for him, and there he saw an old Bible. Opening it, he read this verse *"Call upon me in the day of trouble: I will deliver thee, and thou shalt glorify me."* The Lord spoke to him through that verse. Many of you I am sure can tell of many times the Lord has spoken to you through the Word. That verse is found in **Psalms 50:15**.

HE SPEAKS THROUGH OPEN AND CLOSED DOORS

Again many times when I plan a trip, committing it to the Lord, I would have the door slammed shut. I couldn't understand why I couldn't go. But later down the road I would see clearly why that trip was delayed at that time. On the other hand, when the Lord did open the door for a trip, I could see clearly why He sent me on that trip. It is so wonderful to watch Him work through you. At first we don't realize that he is doing that. Later as we look back we can only praise the Lord for what He is accomplishing through us. It is nothing we do but something that He accomplishes through us. There is no way we can explain it.

HE SPEAKS IN AN AUDIBLE VOICE

I have two incidents where the Lord spoke audibly. the first happened to my son-in-law when he was in the Army and stationed in Florida. He had gone to a Bible study with some of his buddies one Saturday night. The following day, he attended a small church. As the service came to an end he said he heard this audible voice say, "Norbert you are lost." He looked around and knew it wasn't any of the people. He immediately got down on his knees right at his seat and gave his heart to the Lord. The next time he went to the Bible study, the lady that taught it said, "Norbert, you have been saved. I can see it in your face."

As I thought back on his life, I can see that the Lord was preparing his heart along the way, and he was ready to respond. He is past retirement now, but he has served the Lord in preaching (he is an ordained minister), in Christian school work and is a marvelous soul winner. He goes to Hardee's for breakfast and has won many souls to the Lord there. Did you know that Hardee's is a good place to win souls to the Lord? I have another friend in another state that does the same thing since he has retired.

The second incident comes from a testimony given to me.

"In the spring of 1958, God unquestionably called me to full-time service. I was in my car driving up Jefferson Davis Highway toward Richmond. It was one of those times when I was overwhelmed with the joy of knowing Jesus as my Savior. I began thanking Him for all He had done in my life. Then I very joyously thanked Him for allowing me the privilege of teaching young people in Sunday School and serving as a deacon. As I thought on these things, my heart seemed like it was about to jump out of my chest. I said out loud to God, "Is there something else that I can do to show You how grateful I am?" Then an audible voice said, "Emmett, you can preach." That shocked me so much that I immediately pulled my car over to the curb and stopped. 'I must be mistaken,' I thought. The voice must have come from the radio. But there was no radio in my car. It was God answering me. I immediately began to make excuses. 'Lord, you know I cannot preach. I freeze when called on to pray in public. I can't preach. Listen, Lord, I have four children to raise. (Our fourth child, Douglas, had just arrived a few weeks before.) Lord, I just cannot preach.'

I decided to keep that episode quiet. I reasoned that I must have been hallucinating and if I just tried to forget it, it would go away.

Two weeks went by, and I could not forget it. It was with me every waking moment, and I even dreamed about it. Then one evening after our dinner, I went into the living room to watch the news while Betty was cleaning up the dishes in the kitchen. I could not get my mind on the news. I got up and went through the dining room to the kitchen door and said to Betty, "Honey, I have something I have to tell you." Betty turned around, wiped her hands on her apron and ran over to me and put her arms around me and said, "God wants you to preach." All I could do then was to bawl my eyes out. The children came running saying, "'What's wrong with Daddy? We have never seen him cry before.'"

Both of these incidents are written in my second book, ***Precious Memories.*** I would like to go on and finish the stories but time doesn't permit. Just know in both incidents the Lord worked miracle after miracle, and each one went forward with the Lord. Nothing is impossible with God. All he wants from us is a willingness to go forward; and He will do the impossible. I have heard of many that have heard the call to preach. I don't know of any that could immediately say yes. All seem to have a struggle before they can honestly say yes. For you whom God has been trying to call into the ministry, it is not too late. I just heard the story of a man who was a song leader and musician, using his talent for the Lord. His minister died of a heart attack. The people wanted the song leader to be their minister. He was ordained at the age of seventy. He loves his people, and they love him. He said that the Lord had been calling him for many years, but he wanted to pursue his music. He has peace at last. He is a minister, and he still uses his music in the ministry. Our Lord never takes away. He just has something better.

I was rereading the story of Abraham yesterday, and how the Lord called him out of his land to go to a land that He was going to give him. He was supposed to go alone—just he and his wife. But he took his father and his nephew with him. They stopped at Haran. They stayed there until his father died, then went forward. We read of many delays and wrong moves along the way, but finally he comes to the land. Our Lord never holds the mistakes before him but says of his servant, **"Abraham believed God and God counted it unto him for righteousness" (Genesis 15:6.)**

Many times Abraham's faith was weak, but the Lord always encouraged him along the way. When He puts His hand on us for a special ministry, there are going to be times when we get discouraged and feel like giving up, but He is always there to encourage us along the way. The story of Abraham starts in the twelfth chapter of Genesis and covers several chapters. I challenge you to make a study of it. You will really be blessed. In fact, when one makes a study of the book of Genesis, one gets a firm foundation because Genesis is the book of beginnings. Regardless of what subject you are studying, you will find that subject started way back in the book of Genesis.

I have only touched on the subject of God speaking to us. I am sure that many of you are thinking that the Lord spoke to you, but in a different way. One thing is sure: He never speaks anything to anyone that contradicts the Word of God. May the Lord bless you.

Emmett is past retirement age, but is still in the ministry. He is looking to the Lord to lead his future.

Nancy Bell's Testimony

Mrs. Fitzgerald told me that God has given her a hymn for the title of every book she has written. I remember when God gave me a hymn to help me through a trial.

Near the time my second child was born my husband lost his job. What a blow that was! We felt numb, then very anxious. One morning as I was waking up, part of a well-known hymn was going through my mind with heartfelt praise to God. *"All I have needed Thy hand hath provided. Great is Thy faithfulness, Lord, unto me."*

After about ten months, my husband found employment. The Lord was extremely faithful. Here's how:

The same month Dolph lost his job we received some money from a trust fund. We were planning on saving it for future needs, but God had other plans. Our car died a month after the job loss and we were able to buy a new one. With the rest of the money we were able to pay tithe and go through those ten months. We spent all of it, but the *"cruse of oil"* never failed until the *"famine"* was over.

During that time, I feared that I would need to return to work. I had worked in the actuarial profession for four and a half years before the Lord answered my cry and allowed me to stay home with our oldest daughter, then one. I had been at home for two years when this crisis occurred. Full of anxiety, I began to study for another actuarial exam. I remember telling the Lord that what I wanted most of all was to be able to pass some more exams. But in His love, He answered with a better solution. I failed the exam, which hurt my pride. Previously, I had been able to pass exams fairly easily, and the actuarial profession was rated as the number one career to have. But the Lord did not want me to be proud, nor did He want me to return to work.

I studied for and took the exam once more. The day before, I fasted and prayed that God would give me a second chance. That evening my husband handed me a piece of literature that had come in the day's mail and was perfect for witnessing to an old co-worker I was planning to eat lunch with after the exam. The next day I took the exam at my old work place and ran into another person I used to work with. We had been on bad terms, but that day we were able to settle it and I felt such peace! I was able to give the piece of literature to the other co-worker also. I failed the exam again, but I believe that these two events were more important to God than my career and were the "second chances" to do what was right toward others.

There were other signs that I should stop studying for exams and not go back to work. I prayed for guidance. If God wanted me to continue studying, I prayed make it so I do not have to fight for support, but that others will offer to help with the children or encourage me in other ways. I was not going to ask anyone for help. Well no one, including my husband, encouraged me to continue. My old employer was not interested in interviewing me, and I ran into two people during this time who said that they had given up higher education in order to spend more times with their families and never regretted it.

Through all this, God was telling me that He is our provider, although previously I had believed that we were our own providers. What freedom from anxiety to learn this lesson! All we have to do is to seek God's righteousness first, and He promises to care for us (Matthew 6:33).

I believe that God wants wives at home. The marriage roles are upside down if the wife is the provider. Wives are to be the recipients of the husband's care. This is a beautiful picture of Christ and the Church. Our marriage suffered because of me working. God states in Malachi 2:15 that He wants godly children and in Titus 2:5 that women should be keepers at home. I believe that He will enable us to do this no matter how impossible it seems. I John 5: 14,15 says, *"And this is the confidence that we have in Him, that, if we ask anything according to His will, He heareth us: and if we know that He hears us, whatsoever we ask, we know that we have the petitions that we desired of Him."*

Our income has been 1/3 to 2/3rds of what it was before I quit work, yet all of our needs have been met, some better than before, and we now have three children! In the past year, my husband had a pay reduction right at the time our third child was born. Before this happened, my father began sending some money every month to hire a maid since I was about to have a baby and was home schooling. This money which we used mostly for general household expenses, combined with some cuts in unnecessary expenditures, enabled us to go on as before. Dad continued this monthly giving until another miracle happened.

My husband wanted to get his master's degree for quite some time. He and others thought that I would have to work in order for this to occur, but God gave me conviction, support and guidance to refuse to do this. Now the Lord has provided the funds for him to get his master's degree and for me to stay at home with our children, which I am now doing.

During the ten months of unemployment, I prayed for a nicer place to live. I was continually depressed over the ugliness and smallness of our townhouse and concerned that my daughter's playmates were not a good influence on her. I did not pray for a large, magnificent house, but for one with just enough room, that was aesthetically pleasing, with lots of windows and hardwood floors. I also wanted a prayer room. As a young girl, I had told God that if He blessed me with a husband and a home, I would dedicate a special room to Him for prayer. After I married, I did not keep this promise for seven years. Even though He provided us with homes, some of them beautiful. I was not grateful and not living for Him, falling more and more away from Him. Through the unemployment and other problems, He got my attention and drew me back. So now I knew that the house that was, "it" would have a prayer room. We looked around Amherst, where Dolph was newly employed, but could not find any home to rent or buy that would suite us. The home we used to own in Lynchburg was for sale and I wanted so badly to buy it back, but Dolph's boss said for us to live in Amherst. So I reluctantly submitted. After a while we were told of a house to rent in town and we looked at it. It had no extra little room for prayer but I had a peace that this was the house for us. It was just the right size and had plenty of windows and hardwood floors. After moving there, I soon found out that there were wonderful Christian women on the street who have become my good friends. We pray together at my home. I have realized that God doesn't want just one little room. He wants the whole house! These women have daughters the age of mine and are wonderful playmates. My girls have no playmates who are not daughters of wonderful Christian parents. The Lord has led us to many wonderful Christian friends and a good church here. Praise be to Him!

CHAPTER SIX

OUR LORD LONGS TO COMFORT

"Better is little with righteousness than great revenues without right."
(Proverbs 16:8)

  The month of April has been a turbulent month. I wanted to write something about it, but was hesitant to write at this time as it is so recent. I started out with a trip to Chester and Richmond, Virginia. The thing that struck me were the lovely homes I went into. Their owners seem to have anything their hearts desire. I had a lovely time with so many I love, and all were gracious to me. Yet in each home, each had his own burden to carry. The Lord knows just what we can stand, and He never puts more on us than we can bear. I had hardly gotten home, when I heard of my sister-in-law going to be with the Lord. So off I went to Kentucky. While money is no problem with my brother, it could not bring back his wife. While he could have had help with her, he chose to take care of her himself. From there I went to my nephew's home. Again, money was no object, but sorrow was eating away at their hearts because of the loss of a son two years before. The night before we were to come home, we got a call that my oldest son, Larry, had died of a massive heart attack. He had been active all day and dropped dead within fifteen minutes after he got home. Again, money cannot replace the loss of a loved one. For us who know the Lord, the grief is not as bad. He comforts the heart and gives the peace that we may be able to bear it. No matter how much any one has, it can't give us a life free from trouble.

When Mona sent me the verse above, it fit in with my thoughts. The greatest thing we can have is a heart that is right with our Lord. In all these cases, I could see a difference in how the ones who walk with our Lord reacted to their problems. It makes all of us want a closer walk with the Lord. He does something for us we can't understand. Later He uses that in our lives to help us help others along the way. I wish that all could see how alive our Lord is and how He wants to comfort each one along the way. HE IS ALIVE! How much He wants to hold out a helping hand. he knows what suffering is all about, as He suffered far more than any of us will ever be called to suffer.

Another verse that our Lord has given me at this time is *"Blessed is he that considereth the poor: the Lord will deliver him in time of trouble."* **(Psalm 41:1)**

It isn't how much we have that counts. It is how we use it. There are so many who are going through such hard times that a little help along the way means so much to them. Many times we really don't see the need. We are so involved with what we want, and if we notice the troubles of others at all we criticize them, thinking they could have done better. Oh, that the Lord would give us seeing eyes. I think of the man who carried a oil can with him, everywhere he went. Whenever he found a rusty hinge he put a little oil on it to make things smoother along the way. Sometimes just a little lift along the way may be the encouragement that a person needs to cause him to open his heart to the Lord. If the person is a Christian, it gives him a renewed hope as he sees that Jesus does care. Truly, it is more blessed to give than to receive.

The phone just rang. Imagine my surprise to hear the voice of a prisoner to whom the Lord had given me the privilege of writing to for the past two years. He had turned to the Lord. As we corresponded with each other I could see the growth from letter to letter. The Lord led him to form a prayer group and it is going strong. He had been out two days when he called. He told me that he was with the Salvation Army for the next three months, then hoped to go into some kind of program to get established. I am so proud that he has gone with the Salvation Army as he will have someone to encourage him along the way. News like that more than makes up for anything I have done along the way. Pray that he will stay involved. That is the secret of staying close to the Lord. That call made my day. He had struggled so long. It must be terrible to be locked up.

****

I have met many wonderful friends through the books I have written. When someone writes about the book and sends a donation, I write back. It leads to a real friendship. As we write, we seem to help each other. It is a real joy when I see them come through to higher ground for our Lord after they have been going through some trial. (Many I write to have not been able to send donations. The important thing is that the book has been used to help them through a hard time.)

I just received a letter from a friend, We have been writing for some time. The Lord has given her a ministry also. This past year the Lord enabled her to build a house. There was much delay and problems along the way, but, as she says, the Lord built it for them. I had written her to ask her to write something for my last chapter, but had no reply. I got the letter the other day, so will include it in this chapter. I quote in part, "We have moved into the home the Lord provided for us. We were in the midst of our moving when I received the cards. Sorry it has taken me a while to answer.

"I would love to share in the chapter if I'm not too late. you are free to use whatever I share in my letter.

"Our Lord has spoken to me in so many ways. Through His Word, in my spirit, audibly. I remember just before I moved, I heard Him plainly say, 'Joyce, if you would learn to wait on me you would hardly have to buy anything.' He sure has been proving Himself to me. We sometimes move too fast. 'Hurry up, I need it now people.'

"He also told me to step out in faith and I sure have been doing that. In the ministry it takes a lot, but I see the Lord bless in so many ways.

"While the house was being built, the Lord shared

with me from **Romans 8:28.** No matter what goes on in our lives it is working for our good. He also gave me **Jeremiah 33:3.** Call upon Him and He will answer and show me great and mighty things. This He is doing. He is teaching me how to pray. There is so much to learn. I'm taking one day at a time. We need to spend more time with the Lord and seek His face and will for our lives." She signs her letter, Love in Christ, Prophetess Powell. How the joy bells break through with each letter when I see they climb through to higher ground.

****

JIM'S CALL TO THE MINISTRY

    I first met Jim McKinley at our church when we were involved in a missionary meeting. Jim was assigned to us. One day, he and the pastor had lunch with me. What a wonderful time of fellowship we all had together. As we shared, I found that he too had written several books. The Highview Baptist Church in Louisville, Kentucky, had them printed. They handle all the sales of the books. All profits go to the Foreign Mission Board, and are earmarked to be used in Bangladesh. The last I heard, they had $250,000 for the work.

    He now resides in Louisville. While I was in Louisville, I called him. He took the time to come see me. Jim looks so much like my son, Larry, that I felt at home with him. Little did I know that a few days later I would get the news that my son, Larry, had died of a massive heart attack.

    Jim has given me the privilege of going through his third book and relate certain portions to you.

****

JIM MCKINLEY'S TESTIMONY

    I did understand, at the age of sixteen, God wanted me to be a preacher. But every thought of it deeply troubled me. In my understanding, I was everything but a fit subject for such a task. So for four long years, chaos reigned as I struggled with the direction for my life.

But at another high moment, this time with college students from all over Kentucky, we gathered for a Spring Retreat at a camp in Otter Creek Park. We were newly elected Baptist Student Union Council members from our various campuses. This was an attempt to help us understand our special roles for the next college year.

That time ended on Sunday morning. The worship service seemed to reach heaven as far as I was concerned. Or maybe Heaven just reached down to me and others that morning. "Invitation time" came. And in a moment's time, there I was down front talking with the preacher telling him I knew God wanted me to preach, and I wanted to do that.

That preacher, Ernest Brown, later became a foreign missionary. Looking back, I conclude that his counsel to me was near perfection. He said to me, "Your willingness to preach means that you are ready to preach anywhere in the world."

After that beautiful BSU meeting in April 1950, I told my home church, Stony Point Baptist, my decision. I was now one of their "preacher boys". My pastor, O.G. Lawless, responded to my decision with every right word and deed. Following that morning, he was both my pastor and friend.

Aunt Bubba, one of my Sunday School teachers, Mrs. Brice, another teacher and RA leader, Mrs. Violet, one of my Sunday School teachers, and Aunt Viebie, responded with long lasting help for their "preacher boy." All had helped in the formative years of my life.

But there were many others who gave the kind of help I needed. Aunt Nell and Uncle Robert were always encouraging. But standing alone, in their constant support, were my Mom and Dad.

I was to inherit the role of operating the family farm. But it seemed they easily turned loose of that.

JIM'S CALL TO THE MISSION FIELD

I made my way to the College Heights Baptist Church in Plainview, Texas, where I was a member. The church was located just across the road from Wayland. My

Wayland roommate, Franklin Chen, left for his church, a Methodist church in Plainview.

The beginning of this day, I suppose was a normal one. But for me, this changed at my church that Sunday morning during the worship. At "invitation time," it was clear to me that there was no longer any need to wait. I knew that God wanted me to be a foreign missionary. So I moved out into the aisle and made my way toward my pastor, Ralph Reasor, at the front of the church sanctuary.

All doubts about a determined direction for my life were pushed aside. I knew God wanted me to make it clear that He wanted me to be a foreign missionary. I also wanted others in my church to know that I wanted to be one of those missionaries. God had clearly revealed this to me over a long period of time. And now for support, I needed my church. So I shared my feelings and my decision with my pastor. As the gathered worship came to an end, Pastor Reasor told the congregation my decision.

As I walked from the church building to the college dining room, I felt a load had been lifted. Now I could see clearly, concentrate on preparing for the new direction in my life. Even the food in the dining room tasted better. After eating, I quietly walked toward my room in the dormitory. The door was locked. That was unusual. Neither Franklin nor I ever locked it. I didn't even carry my key. I knew that Franklin was inside. I gently knocked and waited. The door clicked; I watched as the doorknob slowly turned. The door opened and there stood Franklin with watery eyes looking directly at me. Then he said, "Jim, that means you will go to China, doesn't it?"

Franklin and I knew the doors to China were tightly closed. My Chinese roommate had great dreams about China in 1952. He was sure those doors would be opened by the time I was ready for missionary appointment.

"Well, you made it, didn't you?" That is what my eldest sister said to me after my appointment as a Southern Baptist missionary to East Pakistan in 1958. As we continued talking she explained that when I was a small boy, I often talked of being a missionary to India. I remembered none of that.

However, East Pakistan, now Bangladesh was a part of India during my childhood. And that is where I spent the best part of my life as a missionary.

Betty and I received our A.A. degrees from Cambellsville College in Kentucky, and became engaged at the close of our time there. We discussed my feelings about being a foreign missionary. We both even then were willing for that to happen.

Then with our ten month old baby, Cherie, we boarded a Dutch freighter in Seattle, Washington. Little did we understand the life of a foreign missionary can be totally fulfilling if you are concerned about making Christ known to some of the world's great people.

Jim tells about visiting a friend of his who had planned to go to the mission field also. He hadn't heard from him for years. One day he received a letter with a news article written by a Chinese student at Southern Illinois University. The article told about his friend, Richard, getting polio. He went to see him and found out that he had been bedridden for years. His wife had died and his mother and brother was taking care of him.

Richard and his mother both had a ministry among the international students. The students came to see him and he tried to lead them to Jesus while they were young. Jim said, "Before the visit ended, I understood that the world had come to Richard and God had sent me to the world. I also understood, in another way, that God's ways are not our ways! I, Jim, had been appointed as a missionary of the Foreign Mission Board of the Southern Baptist Convention for 34 years. Richard and his mother and father, had no less been appointed by God, to be missionaries to foreigners in Carbondale. Richard said it was not difficult to say yes to God about the going but with the staying he had not found it so easy. So through the years, he had struggled with the staying. But his friend Jim, thinks he has "gone and stayed" with his wonderful spiritual ministry.

Though since 1955 Richard had functioned lying on his back, polio had not conquered him, he was not a victim but a victor.

****

BOB CAMPBELL'S TESTIMONY

My brother, Don, is a good Christian man. He made attempts to share the gospel with me to no avail. I would simply become upset with him and walk off. Several visits were made by deacons in my home. They were not impressive and offered nothing of help to me.

A revival was going to be at my brother's church. His son, Donnie, came to invite me to church. A prize would be given to the one who brought the most guests. There were eight in my household, and my nephew would not leave until I agreed to attend.

On the first night of the revival, Donnie came over. We lived right across the road. I could see his house. I said to Donnie, "You had better go home for supper." "Dad said I could eat with you," said Donnie. I continued, "Your folks are getting ready to leave." Donnie said, "Dad said I could go with you."

We attended that first meeting taking my nephew along. We then attended every meeting and attended worship on Sunday. Soon we attended Sunday School, prayer meeting and other meetings. One Sunday morning, I confessed to the preacher, "I don't know this Christ you speak of, but I do know he alone can help me. I accept Him now as my Savior." My wife and two oldest children followed me to the altar and into the baptismal waters.

At my baptism, the Lord called me into the pastoring ministry. I have a son in the ministry, and all of our children and grandchildren are involved in church and good community activities that encourage godliness and good citizenship. I would recommend to all who can read and all who hear this gospel, Christ can and will improve your life and future. You simply must believe in the Lord Jesus Christ. His mission and His call is for <u>you</u>.

****

"SO FAITH COMETH BY HEARING, AND HEARING BY THE WORD OF GOD." (ROMANS 10:17)

When I read this testimony, it brought back so many

precious memories. The church I attended at that time also was having a revival. The evangelist who was holding the meetings was a chalk artist, and the one bringing the most people that night got the drawing. I was a new Christian at that time and was real excited I went out inviting my neighbors. We lived quite a few miles from the church and had to ride a street car. (You see I was old enough to remember them.) One night I won the drawing. The picture that night was a picture of a storm on the ocean with all its fury. There was a lone hand held up like someone was pleading for help. The main song that night was, "I was sinking deep in sin, far from the peaceful shore." And of course the message was all about that subject. At another meeting the man at the same church, who was in charge of the music asked us to try and find some whiskey bottles. He was going to put different amounts of water in them and hang them up like stair steps. He played music on them. I went to a neighbor who I hardly knew (I had heard that he was an alcoholic) and asked him if he had any whiskey bottles and told him what I wanted them for. Would you believe it? He gave me several, and I took them to church. Oh that we would keep that first love that we have when we are first saved! I hope if my Lord would ask me today to do something out of the ordinary, I would still respond. At that church, my daughter and my two sons also made public their decisions to invite Jesus into their hearts. We were all baptized the same night—Betty and I in the pool together and then my two sons, Larry and Bobby, right after us. They had a tract rack in the back of the church. My boys would get a bunch of them and rather than transfer from one car to another, as we went home we would walk down the main street and the boys would each take a side of the street and give tracts to everyone that passed by. There was no doubt that my boys were truly saved. When the boys got older and got away from the Lord, that memory stuck with me. My oldest son came back to the Lord, and I know the younger one will. We have a wonderful Lord! He is precious! And as Brother Campbell said, He will improve your life, and what a joy and peace we have along the way.

Brother Bob is now the pastor of my church,

Ridgecrest Baptist Church. We are fortunate indeed to have such a man of God to lead us.

Larry, the oldest son, is the one that has gone to be with the Lord. Bobby, the younger one is always ready to take me where I have to go when an emergency occurs. He, too, is coming back to the Lord. Our Lord answers prayer!

CHAPTER SEVEN

THE PROMISE BOX

"Behold, I stand at the door and knock: If any man hear my voice, I will come unto him, and will sup with him, and he with me." **(Revelation 3:20)**

Have you ever had a promise box? I mean a real one? One someone has personally made for you? Have you ever taken the time to make one for someone else? I know you can buy one in the form of a loaf of bread with promises on the cards in them. I am not thinking of them.

When I was a new Christian, a lovely Christian lady, who later became a precious friend, took the time to write by hand each promise that had meant so much to her on little pieces of paper, roll them up like a scroll and put them into a little box that she gave to me.

Each morning I would take one as my promise from the Lord for the day. On days when I was going through heavy trials, it seemed that the Lord Himself would give me the very verse I needed to carry me through the day. Not only did I learn the scripture through this, but also learned where to find them in the Bible. The promises became my strength and encouragement.

The other day I went out to the shop to get something and my eyes fell on a promise box I had made for my granddaughter many years ago. What memories it brought back! I had not thought about it for years. I brought the box into the house and placed it on my table and am again enjoying the Lord speaking to me through the verses.

Nancy, my granddaughter, told me that at the time I

sent the promise box she was going through a rough time. The promises are what carried her through. I thought back to that Christmas when the Lord led me to the promise box as a gift. The grandchildren really loved this box, and kept the promises with them through the years. They not only got acquainted with His precious Word, but learned where the verses are in the Bible and can quickly look them up when needed.

Another tradition I have started is making chicken pot holders at Christmas. All who come to my house get one. One of my granddaughters said, "Grandma, if this keeps on I will have to buy a chicken house to put them in."

Now you will want to know, what do chicken pot holders have to do with the Lord? First, I started them for my family. I have six living children and their mates, twenty grandchildren, twenty-five great grandchildren, and three great great grandchildren. You can see the impossibility of buying gifts of any value. But the family keeps the little chickens. Each time they see them it brings back memories of their grandmother and what she stands for as they face decisions in their lives.. Then there are at least forty friends who also add to their collection each Christmas.

We are only here a few years and the most precious gift we can give our children, grandchildren and friends are memories that bring eternal values to mind.

Are you building memories in the minds of your loved ones? What kind? Memories that tear down, or memories that build up? If you look back and feel that you have failed in this, know that our God is the God of second chances. From this day forward purpose in your heart to start building memories in the hearts of your loved ones. As I look back to the time when my children were little, the thing I remembered most was how much I yelled at them. While I included them in all the children's classes, there did not seem to be a pattern in trying to make memories in their lives. I also took them to church. I am talking about the little things that go along with life. Maybe as grandparents we have more time to look back and see where we lacked.

Our Lord brought this to my attention after I had children. We can't undo the past but—praise the Lord—we can put it under the blood, and go forward.

I have a granddaughter who has little children. From the time they were born she has saved things and taken pictures of their grandparents holding them, so as they grow older they will know the ones who have gone on. She is building a rich heritage for them. Another one takes videos of all the important events of her child's life.

From this day, let's start making precious memories for our children. Happy are the children who can look back on a rich heritage, especially if it is in the Lord. The Lord will bring fruit through those memories. I believe it is the little things we do that make a deep impression on our children and grandchildren more than the big things. It is the consistency that counts. Many children experience life like a yo-yo. First up and then down, according to the moods of their parents. Even that can be overcome—if in our hearts we want the Lord to take over and let Him live through us. That is what He wants us to do. Do you want to experience the fullness of the Holy Spirit? If so, look up these verses, read them over and over and pray for the Lord to make them real in your life: **Galations 2:20, Phillipians 2:12-13, Phillipians 3:10.** As we read these verses, we see that it would be an impossibility for any of us to accomplish it. All it requires is a surrender of our wills to Him. He will do the work and bring it to pass.

Let's expose our children to as much Christianity as we can. When one of my grandchildren was going through a very rebellious time during her teen-age years, her daddy took her with him up north to help with rebuilding a church. They were placed with a lovely Christian family. This family took to her and put themselves out to make her stay pleasant. My granddaughter will always remember that lovely couple and she enjoyed pounding nails with the rest of the folks. Later he insisted that she go to a Christian camp, at a time when he had very little. It was a sacrifice to come up with the money. Seemingly, it didn't help much. But one thing was implanted deep on her mind and that was the day a girl gave her testimony. After giving her testimony, the girl said; "One thing I want you girls to remember—if you forget everything else— is that no matter *how deep* in sin you go, Jesus loves you." That was several years ago. She has begun to realize that she needs to start to make something of her life. She has moved back in with her daddy, is going to church, going to college and working on the side. There is much to be accomplished, but praise the Lord the trend has started. Don't give up on your children, no matter how impossible it seems. Remember nothing is impossible with God. The harder the case, the more it glorifies the Lord.

My granddaughter at first lived with her mother through several turbulent years. The mother stayed in prayer and did everything she could to help. She was called on to do things that seemingly turned her daughter off. The daughter hated her mother and plainly told her so. Her mother told me more than once that she knew her daughter hated her and would probably never come to see her again. Her only wish was that her daughter would find happiness again. I told her one day, that the time would come when her daughter would again turn to her. That day is here. She has been to visit her mother on several occasions and calls her all the time.

Mothers, don't be afraid to stand firm with your children. One of the greatest hindrances the Lord encounters is when He is working on our children, and they begin to go through hard times, and we parents want to stretch out our hands to help them so they won't have to go through suffering. In this way, we rob them of Jesus, as we are in the way. It is only through suffering that we really come to know Him in a deep way.

In order for a pearl to form, a foreign object gets into the oyster, and it constantly irritates the oyster. Slowly the pearl is formed. The greater the suffering, the more perfect the pearl.

****

CINDY THOMASON'S TESTIMONY

I had been saved at the age of nine, and knew in my head how important it was to have Christ at the center of my life. But as a working mother and wife, my husband and I were financially stable, and didn't feel the need to rely on anyone but ourselves for our needs. We were healthy, and, as some Christians do, thought that the Lord was not really concerned with our daily actions as long as we didn't hurt anyone.

My grandmother gave us some land to build a home on, and we started to plan, with no thought to what the Lord would have us do. My husband's business was going well, and we thought we would have plenty of money for our new home we were designing. **(Psalm 127:1)**

We didn't know it at the time, but the Lord was planning a wake-up call for us with the building of this house, to get our attention. It is a good thing He doesn't ask our permission first before He wakes us up spiritually.

Seven weeks after we moved into our new home, I had our second daughter, Elizabeth. I wanted to stay home fulltime with her and our three and a half-year old, Emily. My husband's job was going well, so I just quit my job without even a prayer.

Soon after this, our wake-up call started. My husband's business fell apart, and we were unable to make ends meet. I was unable to sleep at night, I was so worried about what would happen to us. My husband and I would fight over nothing; we were so frenzied with worry all the time.

We considered selling our new house, but I couldn't bear the thought having to tell my grandmother the land she had just given us would be sold to strangers. It would have broken my heart to tell her, and I knew it would break my family's heart to hear it.

So I started praying—because I was desperate. I knew deep down that no one else could help. I still remembered that God was in control, even if I hadn't acknowledged it for a long time. My parents helped us financially for awhile. But I knew that if the Lord didn't want us to keep our house, we would not keep it—no matter what earthly help we had.

One day I begged the Lord to show me if we would be able to keep our land and house, because the torment of not knowing was too terrible to bear. To me, anything was better than not knowing if we would need to move or not. The Lord had mercy on me, and showed me a passage,

Ezekiel 34:25-31.
One other time when things were so bleak that we couldn't buy enough groceries, I cried out to the Lord, doubting His promise, and said, "How are we going to be able to stay in this house if we can't even afford groceries?" As patient as He was with Gideon when He doubted, He showed me another passage, **Joshua 21**. Since then I have never doubted that we are here to stay, no matter how bleak things look.

One week, I knew I had to drive to church to do some work I had volunteered to do. I had to go to church on Wednesday. It was Monday when I realized our car was out of gas, and that we didn't have money for gas at all. I got angry with the Lord and said, "How do you expect me to work for You, when You don't provide me with what I need to do it?" I felt that this job was too big even for the Lord. For an answer, later that day a woman called and asked me if I would baby-sit her child on Tuesday. I did, and had money on Wednesday to buy gas. Since then, I have not questioned if He is able to provide us with what we need to do His work (**2 Corinthians 9:8**). I have asked for many things. He always provides us with our needs, and with our wants if they are for our benefit and His glory. I'm still asking for some things that I know are His will, but that are just taking awhile.

I prayed for two more items. Each took over a year to be answered. The first was for a really close Christian friend with whom I could discuss our spiritual journeys. Someone I had barely met during a Bible study had moved away months before, but suddenly started writing to me. We had not written for very long when we realized that only the Lord could have brought us together. When God answered my prayer, He didn't just give us a leftover scrap for a friend. Danelle is the kind of friend worth praying for. She is much wiser and more in tune spiritually, and I know the Lord gave her to me to help me through my rough times.

My second long-term prayer item was for a Christian neighbor. In my neighborhood, people do not move often, so I knew this might take awhile. When a new family moved into my late great-great aunt's house, the Lord kept telling me to visit the new neighbors. After some excuses, I went over. Before I left their house, the woman (Rickie) and I were hugging like long-lost friends and sharing about our faith to each other. I know she will be a good neighbor, because the Lord gave her to me, and He only gives good gifts (**James 1:17**).

I would never have asked for all I have gone through in the past three years, but as I look back, it amazes me how much I have changed, as I let Jesus be in charge. I had made such a mess of my own life that I never want to take charge again. It's as if you're on a long, arduous trip, and you've been driving by yourself, night and day, and no one else can take over. Then you realize you know someone who can and will take over, and you hand the steering wheel over to Him. What a sense of relief I have had, no longer worrying if I will have enough to eat, or if I will have somewhere to stay, or what will become of me (**Psalm 37:25**).

Still, it is our nature as humans to want to take that steering wheel back, so daily I have to pray and read the Bible, to be able to give control back to God, and to find out His will for me for that day.

One week, as I was reading the Bible daily, it occurred to me that no matter what passage I was reading, there would be some reference to "visiting those sick or in prison, feeding the hungry, clothing the naked," etc. I couldn't get that topic out of my head, day or night. Finally I said, "Okay, Lord, if you want me to do some specific work for you, tell me, and I'll do it."

I waited awhile, hoping something would fall into my lap. Nothing happened. I did get a letter from my friend Danelle, urging me to follow up on this. So I figured to be obedient, I needed to set the ball rolling. I wrote a list of all the ministries I could think of, such as prison ministry, soup kitchens, homeless shelters, crisis pregnancy center.

I knew the Lord uses our natural desires, and wants us to enjoy our work for Him, so I decided to try out the only one I had any interest in doing, that being a crisis pregnancy center. I had heard of people counseling for it, but I knew that was not for me. When I called the center, I had no clue how this could relate to me or my talents, but when I talked to a director, she mentioned that they had been praying desperately for a childbirth education teacher. Suddenly I knew without a doubt that this was where the Lord wanted me. He had been so patient to guide me slowly, so I could follow. It is thrilling to know that the Creator of the universe wants me in a specific job, and that I can be of use to Him.

Some people believe that it is enough to be saved, and then coast on that for the rest of their lives. It's true that you cannot lose your salvation, but if you really want God to bless you and help you grow, there must be some "fruit" or work you do for Him because of what he has done for you **(James 2:14-26)**. If you really want to grow in Christ, ask, and He will show you where He wants you.

CHAPTER EIGHT

GOD WANTS TO DEAL WITH LOVE

"If my people, which are called by my name, shall humble themselves, and pray, and seek my face, and turn from their wicked ways: then I will hear from heaven, and forgive their sin, and will heal their land."

(II Chronicles 7:14)

    I have a prayer diary, and on the last page I have the above verse to pray for our land. As I would come to that verse, I couldn't get past it. I had heard a man say that if God doesn't send judgment on America, then He owes the world an apology. And I guess I in a different way was saying, the Bible plainly says that in the last days things would get worse. But each time I came to it I again would say to the Lord, "You know what you predicted, how can I pray against Your will. I honestly needed to know, and as I talked to the Lord about it, He brought to my attention the story of Jonah. Here we have a man God called to do a specific job, but instead of obeying God he ran in the opposite direction. How many of you reading this book have felt a call from the Lord but have turned away from it?
    However, God was not through with Jonah. He ran in the opposite direction and boarded a ship and went down in the hole and fell fast asleep. God sent a terrific storm where all on board were in danger. The sailors were working hard to save the ship, all the time calling out to their gods to save them. Things continued to get worse, so the captain awoke

Jonah and wanted to know why he wasn't calling on his God. Jonah revealed that he was running away from His God. When they wanted to know what they could do, he told them they would have to throw him overboard. The sailors feared Jonah's God and tried in every way to bring the ship to land. They finally knew that they would have to throw him overboard to save their lives. They asked Jonah's God not to lay upon them innocent blood. Even the heathen are often made to realize the true God when something like this happens.

God was not through with Jonah. So He prepared a great fish to swallow him. Did you know that one day some men were fishing, and they caught a large fish. When they were dressing it, they found a man inside that was still alive. There was a story about it in the paper at the time. Could it be the Lord let it happen to say to an unbelieving world that God still controls the world?

I am sure that Jonah had prayed to the Lord many times, but now he really prayed! He was at the one place that his only hope was God. He knew that he was helpless. God had at least gotten his attention, and as he prayed, the Lord answered and gave him another chance to obey Him. Jonah went from being a disobedient Christian to being an afflicted one. From there, he turned to the Lord in prayer, and God heard his cry and the fish took him toward Nineveh and vomited him up on dry ground. And God again told him to go to Nineveh and preach the message, He had told him to preach. He reluctantly went. He must have been a sight after three days in the belly of that fish. As he came to Nineveh, he began walking through the city calling out, "Within forty days Nineveh will be overthrown. He cried out over and over again. It took three days to walk across the city. Because he finally obeyed the Lord, a whole nation was saved. Our God is merciful. He gives us every chance to change our ways before He sends His judgment. If we don't yield to His love, we must yield to His pressure. Jonah missed the blessing because he did not go willingly.

If we are truly followers of God, we have been put in places that our only hope is God. Some people call it wits-end corner. Where we turn completely to God or turn our backs on Him. Is God calling you to do something that you are rebelling against? What will be the outcome if you fail to do it? Will there be people who will never hear the gospel, that only you could reach? Maybe it is that neighbor that the Lord has been picking on you to go see and you keep putting it off. Maybe it is a letter He would have you write. No matter how small or large, if it is not done there are many losers along the way.

There are two incidents that I want to mention, as the Lord has brought them to mind. The first one is in regard to really praying. There was a man who loved the Lord. Every evening when he came home from work, he would go to his large chair in the living room, read his Bible and have his prayers. One night when he came home, he was greeted with the news his daughter was dying. That night he really prayed.

The second incident was when Corrie Ten Boom got out of prison in Germany. She went everywhere talking of God's forgiveness and His love. She told the Lord that she would go anywhere He wanted to send her, but to Germany. The Lord wants full obedience so He sent her to tell the German people of His love and forgiveness. This was a real test because the Germans were the people who had been so cruel to her family and her. It isn't too hard to go to others and talk about this, but to go before your enemies, ones that have hurt you so much, is not the easiest thing to do. It was a real test of her loyalty to her God. Our Lord had a precious lesson to teach her. There she stood giving out the message of God's love and forgiveness to all people who repent, regardless of what they had done.

She mentioned Ravensbrook, the prison she had been in. After the meeting was over, a man started to walk toward her. He did not recognize her, but as she saw him coming, she recognized him as one of the cruelest guards there. The picture came before her face of the terrible beatings that he gave her sister Betsie. She felt like she had died inside herself at that moment. He came up and told her how much her message meant to him as he had been a former guard at the camp that she mentioned. he knew the Lord had forgiven him but he wanted to ask her forgiveness on behalf of all the ones he had mistreated. All of her called out inside her saying no, no, no. But she knew that if she wanted to serve her Lord she had to forgive. With no feeling at all she reached out her hand. As their hands met, God's forgiving love was there, and both felt the healing. This is what **Galatians 2:20** tells us. This is what he wants for every believer: *"I am crucified with Christ, nevertheless I live; yet not I, but Christ liveth in me."* Many things that we go through, the Lord uses to help us understand others and helps us stand by them as they are called to go through deep trials.

    Now to get back to the verse we first started with. In my morning's reading, I read the story of Josiah. He followed the reign of some of the wickedest kings. He wanted to do what was right in the sight of the Lord. The priest, while getting the money out of the chest to give to the workmen who were repairing the House of the Lord, found the book of the law and brought it to Josiah. When he read the book and saw how far all had drifted away from the law, he was grieved. He immediately sent the book to the prophetess Hulda so she could inquire of the Lord about it. Hulda sent word that indeed all that he said would happen. But he told her to tell Josiah, *"Because thine heart was tender, and thou hath humbled thyself before the Lord, when thou heardest what I spake against this place and against the inhabitants thereof that they should become a desolation and a curse, and hast rent thy clothes, and wept before me: I also have heard thee, saith the Lord. Behold therefore, I will gather thee before thy fathers, and thou shalt be gathered unto thy grave in peace. And thine eyes shall not see the evil which I will bring upon this place. (II Kings 22:19,20)* As I began to think about this portion of Scriptures, I could see that the Lord does not want to bring judgment on anyone. And when He sees that we are in earnest in our prayers as we humble ourselves before Him, He will hear from heaven and answer them. *"When two or three are gathered together in my name I am in the midst of them."* (Matthew 18:20)

I believe if we band together in prayer, the Lord will send a real revival, a Holy Ghost revival, that will get hold of people and many will turn their hearts in full surrender to our Lord. I believe we will see the prayers that we have prayed through the years answered.

In one of my devotions this morning, I came across this:

"We must keep on praying and waiting upon the Lord, until the sound of a mighty rain is heard. There is no reason why we should not ask for large things; and without a doubt we shall get large things if we ask in faith, and have the courage to wait in patient perseverance upon Him, meantime doing those things which lie within our power to do.

"We cannot create the wind, or set it in motion, but we can set our sails to catch it when it comes. We cannot make the electricity, but we can stretch the wire along upon which it is to run and to do its work; we cannot in a word, control the spirit, but we can so place ourselves before the Lord, and so we do the things He has bidden us do, that we will come under the influence and power of His mighty breath."

Our part is to be obedient to whatever the Lord asks us to do. He will take care of the results for us. Praise His name!

Some years back, I received a letter written from a summer missionary to the Indians in South Dakota. She had sent for my book before leaving that summer and had forgotten all about it. When she arrived home, the book was waiting for her. After reading it, she wrote me a letter filled with many questions. The way the letter ended, I realized that the Lord was speaking to her about something, and that she probably didn't realize herself what it was all about. I answered her questions as best I could. We formed a real friendship through our letters, Behind the scene was LeRoy, her husband. He always signed his name, "Prayer Warrior LeRoy." I am so grateful that they bear me up in prayer every day. He is also a living witness for his Lord. I will try and fill you in with what I have picked up on the way. If she will write a testimony, I will include it at the end of this.

LeRoy worked for a railroad for years. One day he was injured and was put on disability. They lost their home and all financial security. Through this they were drawn closer to the Lord. LeRoy says, "if it hadn't been for this, I would have never entered the intercessory prayer ministry." She seems to be more outgoing. He is quieter, but he is constantly in prayer to his Lord.

They would save all they could through the winter, collect clothing, and in the summer would drive to the Indian reservation with their trailer bulging. They would spend the summer working among the Indians. During the last few years, the door seemed to be closed. When they did get to go back, they went in late fall. The Lord has kept them warm and well. They intend to stay as long as the Lord wants them there. The last letter I received, just a few days ago, told how the Lord was blessing the work and how it was going forward. As an afterthought she added, "There seems to be a hate campaign going on toward the white people bringing up what they did to the Indians one hundred years ago. It was in the paper that one white man was killed and two white women were raped and left for dead. Lisa, my daughter, is married to an Indian and she said, "Mama, it seems like they are trying to push us out."

When a real work of God is going on, Satan always tries to destroy it. Since I have been writing them, I will mention some of the things they have been through. Shortly after we began writing, her father, who was a Pentecostal preacher, stopped at a service station and dropped dead of a heart attack. He had just left her house. As she was very close to her father, it hit her pretty hard. Their daughter was kidnapped by a boyfriend, she was trying to break from. Her boyfriend had asked her to walk to the park so they could talk things out. She went like she was, as it wasn't far. He had parked his car around the corner. He forced her into the car and took off. He kept her in the car and just rode for days. When word got around, we were all praying. He finally let her out of the car and somehow she found her way back to the house. Our prayers were answered. Our Lord had His protection around her, and she was not harmed in any way. For a time, it seemed that Loretta had people come to stay until they could get located. They would be there for quite a while before moving. It was very hard as she lived on a very limited income. The day her dryer was repossessed seemed to be the last straw. When I received her letter, I wrote back and told her that she would see the hand of the Lord at work. And about two weeks later, the Lord opened the door for them to go to the Indian reservation as full-time faith missionaries. She has always had many problems with her health. Since the day they arrived she has had perfect health, even though they are always going into homes ministering to the sick. Our Lord is good!

When Lorreta came to that place that she was not only willing to go full-time, but was eager to work among them the Lord worked it all out. For her the dryer brought the climax. In my case, it was the washing machine. I will never forget that morning I cried to the Lord and told Him if He could do anything with my life He could have it. He heard that cry, and I am so thankful that He did.

Since Loretta has turned is all over to the Lord, He is working among her children. She was concerned about leaving her youngest daughter. The daughter has gotten married and living closer to her husband's work. Her son had been talking about committing suicide. he is now saved, and his live-in girlfriend also got saved. They are now married and are bringing their children up for the Lord. He has moved closer to his brother so he can witness to him. When we answer the call, we can leave our loved ones in the hands of the Lord.

I received a letter from her and will quote it as she wrote it:

LEROY AND LORETTA HELM'S TESTIMONY

"As I read your letter, I thought you did a good job. Lori's new husband is a minister in the Lord, and Greg and his family are doing very well. Praise the Lord! Lisa and her family are fine and coming to services once in a while, getting back to God. Praise the Lord!

We received a letter from our oldest son this past week, and God has truly kept him safe this week! He has one of those Jeep-like "cars." I'm not sure the name of it, but it's small, and he goes four wheeling in it. he was coming home from work, pulling a trailer he had built himself as he is a welder by trade. He went to make a right, to go into the country road that they live on, when a man came following up behind him, driving 55 m.p.h. and crashed into his rear end. Truly God had His hand on our son! The crash pushed the trailer up underneath the vehicle, completely tore out the gas tank and everything else under there, totaled the trailer and the vehicle and the only injury David got was a sore neck! Oh, how we praise and thank the Lord! If not for God, I am sure the gas tank would probably have exploded with our son inside the vehicle! It always pays to pray for our loved ones. LeRoy is my backbone, a quiet person who truly loves the Lord! He has to be the most patient man I've ever known and has tremendous faith in our God! I am just the opposite. I talk a lot, plain spoken, when sometimes I should keep my mouth shut! I'm also a worry-wart and very impatient. I want everything done yesterday! I have faith in God, but I've had a real battle learning to completely trust Him, without wavering in my faith. I've had a real battle, overcoming worry, especially when it comes to money and things needed to be done or repaired and there is no money! But praise God, with the Lord's help, teaching me, guiding me, I have finally overcome those battles and no longer find it hard to let go of problems and REALLY trust God to take care of them!

    LeRoy worked for the Chicago-Rock Island-Union Pacific Railroad until it went bankrupt and closed down. He was injured on another job. When Rock closed, I thought my world had ended. We had raised four children in a big two-story house in Kansas City, Kansas. We filled that big house with brand new, nice furniture and appliances. LeRoy made good money, and we ate well. But we were lost without God! Always there was something missing in our lives. We had two nice cars, money to go on nice vacations, or to places in the city, and out to eat often. We thought we had it made, but still a void was there. The first thing to be repossessed was all that beautiful furniture. I can still remember LeRoy standing in the living room his head hung down, as the men carried out our nice furniture. I sat on the staircase, with our four babies crying my heart out, as our children watched, looking very puzzled. With each piece the men carried out, my heart seemed to break more and I began to receive bitterness, hatred and such anger in my heart. Our neighbors were standing on their porches or in their yards, watching. I can still feel the shame and the embarrassment I felt that day. It didn't take long for every piece of furniture to be emptied out of our house. Instead of turning to God, as I had been raised to do, I turned from Him more, so hurt and bitter, blaming Him for something I felt He had done to us. We lived in that house (empty) until a friend gave us a table with no chairs and a sofa. They looked awfully lonely in that big empty house. I became depressed to the point that I didn't want to live any longer. Our eldest daughter, Lisa—only thirteen years old–attempted suicide, but failed, praise God! Because of her attempt, the state of Kansas took her from the hospital. We didn't know where she was for three months. We had no idea she was taken until we went to visit her at the hospital and found she was gone. It took us over a year to get her back. I'm getting ahead of myself, though. Anyway, the next thing we lost was our family car, a nice station wagon. We had struggled for a year, went hungry many, many times to try to keep our house. We sold the car to make a house payment. LeRoy had been hurt. We had to go to Social Services, and they gave us a little over $200 a month in money and almost $200 in food stamps. I was as low as I could go! Never had we dreamed we'd have to turn to welfare, and it was a bitter pill to take. But we had three children to feed. Lisa had been taken away, so we swallowed our pride and used food stamps. I'm not against such things, but I was full of pride and didn't have to accept charity before, so it was rough! When I watched the man drive our car off, I cried more tears and became more bitter, turning from God even more. A few short months later, the bank repossessed our house, the home we loved and had lived in so long. I thought it had hurt to watch our furniture being taken out and to see our car driven off, but really didn't know what pain was until we had lost Lisa, then the house. All the while, my minister dad was telling us we better turn to God. But I was too bitter. I couldn't. LeRoy is from Missouri so we decided to move there, in hopes of a better life. He began to serve the Lord and change his life around and prayed for me to do the same. Life in Missouri wasn't any easier. In fact, it was worse. We spent many long, lonely and very hungry days there. One day God dealt with my heart, and I turned to Him instead of away from Him, as I had been doing for so long. The bitterness just rolled from my heart, along with the anger and hatred I'd felt for so long. I truly believe the Lord brought Sister Josephine into my life. She has been and continues to be such a blessing to us and a big help—both spiritually and naturally. When I read her first book, I was amazed at how God brought her through and how similar our circumstances were in life.

I thank and praise the Lord for saving me, calling us into His work bringing us through so many struggles, hardships and tests and trials. I believe with all my heart that if it wasn't for the things we have gone through, there would still be an emptiness in our lives. We would not be serving the Lord or have happiness. We have learned that neither money nor material things bring happiness and love. Only living for and serving our Lord Jesus Christ can do that. I'd rather have Jesus than all the houses, fine furniture and cars that money can buy! Now we are laying up treasures in heaven. Praise God!

We are currently living on Rosebud Sioux reservation in South Dakota, working for the Lord and will remain here until the Lord sends us somewhere else. We praise and thank the Lord for all he has done for us, and we thank Sister Josephine for giving us the opportunity to tell a little bit of what God has done in our lives. We have much to be thankful for. Praise God!

****

That was the end of the testimony part, but she included the following part about the work they are doing. "I was called to a lady's house at almost midnight to pray. She had the flu, strep throat and an ear infection and had been to the doctor that morning for a shot of penicillin. LeRoy and I prayed for her, and she seemed to grow worse with extremely high fever. She was talking out of her head and thrashing around on her bed, fighting her husband, thinking that he was trying to harm her. He was at his wit's end. He had two babies, ages one and a half and five months old. Both were crying, and he didn't know what to do. I told him just to pray and asked him to get me some olive oil. He didn't understand but he did so. LeRoy and I blessed it, prayed for the girl again and LeRoy asked permission to anoint and to bless their little home. The man said, "Do anything to help my wife." As LeRoy went about rebuking the devil and blessing the house, I sat on the chair beside the girl and continued to pray for her. We sat there until three in the morning, but God healed her. She got up and said "Thank you" to us and "I'm hungry" to her husband. She had not eaten for several days. She wanted oatmeal, and she got off her sick bed, went to the kitchen and cooked all of us oatmeal at about 3:30 a.m. We were exhausted when we got home, but were happy, rejoicing in the Lord for bringing her off a bed of sickness! Glory to God! Truly he is still a healer and worthy of all praise, and glory and honor!

CHAPTER NINE

HOW ISRAEL CAME INTO BEING

"YE HAVE NOT CHOSEN ME, BUT I HAVE CHOSEN YOU, AND ORDAINED YOU, THAT YE SHOULD GO AND BRING FORTH FRUIT, THAT YOUR FRUIT SHOULD REMAIN: THAT WHAT SO EVER YE SHALL ASK OF THE FATHER IN MY NAME, HE WILL GIVE YOU."
(John 15:6)

When I was fifteen years old I talked my mother into letting me quit school and get a job. I had attended a small private school through the eighth grade. We move to a large city and for the first time I entered a public school. I felt so all alone and was perfectly miserable. After a while my mother agreed to let me quit school and I started looking for a job. I found temporary work in an office. The place was run by Jewish people. When Good Friday came around, our boss said that all Catholic people could get off to go to church. When I left he wanted to know what a Jewish girl was doing going to a Catholic church. He thought I was Jewish. I hadn't thought of that in years.

Several years ago I received a prayer diary that I began to use each day during my prayer time. One of the prayer request was, *"Pray for the peace of Israel, for they shall prosper that love thee"*. I would always wonder how to pray, other than just saying these words over and over. One day I received a prayer list in the mail with several prayer request on it. The prayer list came from Israel from the Messianic Jewish Faith, a ministry that seeks to convince Jewish people that Jesus is the true Messiah. Jews are not guaranteed heaven any more than gentiles. While they were chosen especially by God, they too must come through the Messiah, our Lord Jesus Christ, the only one. In the gospel of John chapter 14:6 it says, *"I am the way the truth and the life, no one comes to the Father but by me."*

Way back in Genesis 3: 14,15, the Lord is speaking to Satan and He says; *"So the Lord God said to the serpent, because you have done this you are cursed more than all cattle, and more than every beast of the field; and on your belly you shall go, and you shall eat dust all the days of your life. And I will put enmity between you and the woman and between your seed and her seed; He shall bruise your head, and you shall bruise his heel."* In these verses, first He was speaking to the serpent who let Satan speak through him. We can see that today when you see a snake, their markings are beautiful but they are deadly. They have to crawl on their bellies, and they do eat the dust of the ground. Then He goes a little deeper and speaks to Satan. He tells him that although he will bruise the Lord's heel, in the end the Lord will bruise his head. A very vital part of the body. So, no matter how much Satan tries to make us believe he is in control, we know that our Lord has the last say and Satan will be no more.

In Genesis, we have our first shedding of blood. The Lord had to kill a lamb and make clothes of skin to hide the nakedness of Adam and Eve. As we go into the fourth chapter, we see that the children had been taught to offer up a blood sacrifice at a certain time. The day Cain decided to offer up the works of his hands instead of the blood sacrifice required by God, he made his choice. He wanted to worship the Lord in his own way. Adam and Eve both tried to cover themselves in fig leaves, and the Lord had to show them the correct way to worship him. When the Lord accepted Abel's offering and refused Cain's offering, the Lord gave Cain another chance. But rather than accept it, he killed his brother in anger. All Christian parents want their children to accept the Lord and pray that the day will come when their children will make their own decision to follow the Lord. That is a choice they have to make. We cannot make it for them, as God has given each one of us a free will. The choice is theirs.

"Without the shedding of blood, there is no remission of sin." (**Hebrews 9:22**) There is no further account of any following the Lord until we come to verses 25, 26 which says, *"And Adam knew his wife again; and she bare a son, and called his name Seth,' for God said she; hath appointed me another seed instead of Abel, whom Cain slayed'. And to Seth, to him was also born a son; and he called his name Enos. Then began men to call upon the name of the Lord."*

When we come to the seventh generation from Adam we have the birth of Enoch. It tells us that when Enoch was sixty-five years old he begat a son and called him Methuselah. I read somewhere that the name means *"When he dies it shall be sent."* Enoch did not walk with the Lord until after he had this son. Did God reveal a secret to Him? Did that name mean that judgment was to fall when Methuselah died? I am sure that Enoch watched over him closely. After that Enoch walked with the Lord for 300 years, then God took him. He and Elijah seemed to be the only two that didn't experience death.

As we follow the story, we see that Methuselah lived longer than any other man, and died just before the flood. Doesn't that show the longsuffering of our Heavenly Father? In **II Peter 3:9** we read, *"The Lord is not slack concerning His promise, as some men count slackness; but is longsuffering to us-ward, not willing that any should perish but that all should come to repentance."*

At the time of Enoch's death the whole world had turned to sin—only one light shining. Chapter 6: 8,9b says, *"But Noah found grace in the eyes of the Lord. Noah was a just man and perfect in his generation and Noah walked with God."* Have you ever felt you were the only one who was standing for God? Remember how the Lord told Elijah, when he felt that he was the only one, that He still had 7,000 who had not bowed their knees to Baal? Noah was really standing for His Lord alone. I think of that verse in **Acts 16: 30,31,** talking about the Phillipian jailer: And they said, *"Believe on the Lord Jesus Christ, and thou shalt be saved, and thine house."* While it doesn't tell us much about his sons, they too were taken aboard the Ark and saved from the flood.

The Lord moved Noah to build a boat, and it took 120 years to complete it. All the world saw Noah building that boat, far up on the mountain, far from any body of water. As it had never rained at that time they thought that Noah was touched in the head. I can see it now. Here he is obeying what the Lord told him to do. Even he must have wondered; he had never seen rain either. At that time the Lord watered the earth by sending dew on the ground. I am sure with all the persecutions, Noah still tried to warn the people. Not one listened to him. The day came when the boat was finished, and the Lord had Noah put the animals and his family in the boat or Ark. <u>Then the Lord shut the door.</u> Then the rain began to fall. I am sure that many of them tried to get on the boat then, but it was too late, as the Lord Himself had shut the door. Forty days and forty nights the rain came down. Then they had to wait until it was safe to get off the boat. When it was time to come off the boat, they built an altar and worshipped the Lord. A cleansed earth, a new beginning. Now that there were no challenges, Noah started to plant a vineyard. As time went on I guess he began to forget the Lord and the sin of drunkenness came in. It led to the sin of one of his sons. We don't hear much more about him after that, only that all peoples are descendants of his three sons. The Jewish race can be traced back to Shem. The Gentiles to Japhet. And the dark-skinned people to Canaan, the son of Ham.

Noah started out so strong, and when the challenges were gone, he drifted into sin. May we always pray that we won't drift away from the Lord as we grow older. Also help us to remember when we drift away from the Lord that some of our children may never come to the Lord.

After Noah, the people multiplied and decided to build a tower that would reach up to heaven. They didn't see a need for God. When the Lord saw that, He confused their language so they couldn't understand each other. So the people began to gather with the ones that they could understand. And that is where the different languages came from.

At this time the land was in complete darkness, no one was walking with the Lord. Nothing is impossible with the Lord, He appeared to a man named Abram, in the land of Ur of Chaldees and told Abram to leave his fathers' house and come to a land that He would show him. He was to come alone, just he and his wife. While Abram did leave, he brought his father and nephew with him. His father's name was Terah, which means *"delay"*. They got as far as Haran and there stayed until his father died. Later we see all the problems that Lot, his nephew brought on him. It pays to give our Lord complete obedience. We, like Abram, go through much heartache when we only obey Him partially. Our Lord is so patient with us. We should remember that when others are going through their things not to judge but to bear them up in prayer.

Later, the Lord promised Abram that he and Sarai would have a son. It was many years later, but the Lord kept His promise, and when Abram was 99 years old the Lord appeared to him again. He changed his name to Abraham and Sarai to Sarah. And again God told them they were to have a son and were to call his name Issac, which means *"laughter"*. When Abraham was 100 and Sarah was 90 years old, Issac was born. Oh, so much happened along the way, I long to share it all, but want to bring you to the way the nation Israel was formed. The book of Genesis is a wonderful study. All who will take the time to study it will receive a rich blessing.   Issac grew up and married Abraham's brother's child, Rebecca. She conceived and bore twins, Esau and Jacob.

As far as children go, many times Esau may have been seen as the best child, as the world standards go. But deep inside Jacob seemed to have a love for spiritual things. While the Lord had to allow Jacob to go through many things, it was his twelve sons the Lord used to form the nation Israel.

Isn't that so much like us? We take Him into our lives and while we are different than before we were saved, we still try to control our lives until one day we come to *"wit's end corner"*, where we know it is God or else, as we have made such a mess of our lives. When you come to that place if you will only let go and let God you will wonder why you held back so long.

Now why was the nation Israel brought into being? What was the purpose of it? You see, with all the world in darkness, the Lord needed someone to show the world that there was a true God. He didn't choose the Jews for anything good in them, but purely to work His miracles for them, that the world watching would see that they worshipped a God Who took care of them, one who was all powerful. By seeing this, they too would want Him to be their God. Why the Jews? He chose them because they were fewer in number. In **Deuteronomy 7: 6-8** our God says, *"For thou art an holy people unto the Lord thy God: The Lord thy God hath chosen thee to be a special people unto Himself, above all the people that are upon the face of the earth. The Lord did not set His love upon you, nor choose you, because you were more in number than any people; for ye were the fewest of all people: But because the Lord loved you, and because He would keep the oath which He had sworn unto His fathers, hath the Lord brought you out with a mighty hand, and redeemed you out of the house of bondage from the land of Pharaoh King of Egypt."*

One day I heard someone tell a friend of mine, when she asked him how to pray for Israel, that when we pray for Israel we are praying for ourselves as we are the spiritual Israel. We are in the church age, and we form the bride of Christ. Why did our Lord choose us for His bride? In chapter 1 of **I Corinthians 13-25,** Paul addresses the Corinthian church, which was exulting in human wisdom, which is foolishness in the eyes of God: *"For the preaching of the cross is to them that perish foolishness, but unto us which are saved it is the* *power of God. For it is written, I will destroy the wisdom of the wise, and will bring to nothing the understanding of the prudent. Where is the wise? Where is the scribe? Where is the disputer of this world? Hath not God made foolish the wisdom of this world? For after that in the wisdom of God the world by wisdom knew not God, it pleased God by the foolishness of preaching to save them that believe. For the Jews require a sign, and the Greeks seek after wisdom: But we preach Christ crucified, unto the Jews a stumbling block, and unto the Greeks foolishness; But unto them which are called, both Jews and Greeks, Christ the power of God, and the wisdom of God. Because the foolishness of God is wiser than men; and the weakness of God is stronger than men."* Then we go to verses 26-28, *"For ye see your calling, brethren, how that not many wise men after the flesh, not many mighty, not many noble are called: But God hath chosen the foolish things of the world to confound the wise; and God hath chosen the weak things of the world to confound the things which are mighty; and the base things of the world and things that are despised, hath God chosen, yea the things which are not, to bring to nought the things that are, that no flesh should glory in His presence."* That doesn't give us much to get puffed up about. When we begin to see ourselves maybe just a little further along than our brother, we need to think back to what we were when the Lord first started working on us. We should say, *"There but for the grace of God go I."* Another scripture in **I Peter 2: 9, 10** says, *"But ye are a chosen generation, a royal priesthood, an holy nation, a peculiar people; that ye should show forth the praises of Him who hath called you out of darkness into His marvelous light: Which in times past, were not a people, but are now the people of God: which had not attained mercy, but now have obtained mercy."*

In concluding this chapter I want us to see that none is saved except through the blood of Christ. In order for a Jew to be saved he needed to realize that there was a messiah coming and look forward to the time He would come. In those days the people around the Jews who wanted what they had joined them in worshipping the true God. While they looked forward to the cross, we look back to the cross. None can come unto the Father except through the blood of the Lamb that taketh away the sins of the world. Open to all who will repent and believe, Jew or Greek.

CHAPTER TEN

IN THE MIDST OF TRIALS THERE ARE THOSE OASIS IN THE DESERT

"God is our refuge and strength: a very present help in time of trouble." **(Psalms 46:1)**

June had hardly begun until I got word that my youngest son, Tom, was having heart problems. As he wasn't sure about his insurance, he almost waited too long before going to the hospital. He had just changed jobs about two months before and had not put in for the insurance there. In checking with his old employer, he found out that the insurance there, was good until July 1st. He immediately checked into the hospital, and they began running tests. His daughter, Angie, called and informed us he was to have heart surgery the following Monday.

My son, Bobby, called me, and we made plans to leave the next day (Saturday) taking Tom's two younger daughters (who lived with their mother) with us. As Tom lived in Miami, we had a long drive ahead of us. We drove all the way to Brunswick, GA, that day, arriving around 10:30 that night. We checked into a motel and then went out to eat, so it was late before we got to sleep. The next morning, after eating breakfast, we left around 9:30. We drove pretty steady and arrived at the hospital around 6 p.m.

The following morning, he had the surgery. The doctors went in thinking that they were going to do a triple by-pass, but instead he had to have a quadruple by-pass. The doctors and nurses there were wonderful. And praise the Lord all went well. He wasn't in the hospital much more than a week. They informed him that if the slightest thing went wrong, he was to call the hospital and they would send a nurse to the house. I just received a letter from him telling me that all was going well with his heart.

As we left to return home, we decided to take our time and turn it into a vacation for the two girls. This was their first time in Florida. Our first side trip was to Cape Canaveral where we watched the shuttle take off. Then Bobby took me to a friend's house in Mt. Dora, while he and the girls spent two nights in Orlando. He took them to Disney World, and they had a ball.

The friend I went to see was Ruth Fidenger. All of you who read my second book, *"Precious Memories"*, will remember that Ruth found a copy of my first book, *"When thou passeth through the waters"*, in a Kroger store as she and her husband were traveling. She doesn't even remember what town they were in. She called me, and as we talked on the phone she told me she had been going through a dry spell in her Christian life. I suggested that maybe we would correspond and have Christian fellowship through letters. She was delighted, as they were on the road so much she rarely got to attend church at the time. In all the years we wrote, I was getting to meet her in person. That visit was my *"oasis"* in the desert. Ruth planned many things, and we packed a week into two days. She took me to meet many people and several churches. As I talked to various ones, I was thrilled to see how the Lord has used her. One special place she took me to was Hampton Dubose Academy and meeting Evelyn Stone. It was special because I had several friends that had attended that school and at that time I had prayed and kept up with the news there. The wonderful thing is that Ruth is unaware of it all. She just loves the Lord and can't help bubbling over.

During the time we wrote, Ruth was surely put to the test. If I wrote it all down, it would take some time. The man she was married to, was her second husband. This man abused her, and the day came when he put her out. She went to a shelter called *""the Anthony House"*. The Lord was with her and in a short time arranged a place for her to go to. Now she ministers to the people there. Ruth is a caring person, and her heart goes out to anyone in need. While there she gave me the following testimony. It had been written right after the death of her first husband.

Ruth Fidenger's Testimony

Before I received the gift of eternal life I hadn't given much thought to my daily life. Like the white soap that floats, it had a lot of good qualities. God didn't expect us to be perfect. There were plenty of people that weren't trying as hard as I was.

One thing bothered me though—I hadn't found real joy. My enthusiasm for new things dwindled about the time the first coupon came off the payment book. I read every magazine that promised happiness. It seemed like a deep hunger, craving something, and never knowing what. People thought I was happy, but this lack of joy became my most carefully hidden secret.

One day I met some people who had real joy in their lives. Through association with these people I discovered I could have it too. I was willing to do whatever that was necessary. That was the turning point in my life. After I received the gift of eternal life, everything began to take a new meaning and quality. Personal goals no longer depended on financial success. If my best efforts failed, and I were left with nothing, I knew I still had something of greater value.

Then suddenly tragedy struck. My husband died. My mind was electrified with the pain of loss and of decisions I would have to make without him.

But wonder of wonders, like a summer breeze a most amazing peace swept over me, and I sensed the presence of a Holy God and the deep meaning of His everlasting promise to "never leave nor forsake me."

Now I know I will see loved ones again when the cares of this world are past. It's good to know I am going to heaven when I die.

CHAPTER ELEVEN

CHANGING A BURDEN TO A SONG

"Speaking to yourselves in psalms and hymns and spiritual songs, singing and making melody in your heart to the Lord; giving thanks always for all things unto God and the Father in the name of our Lord Jesus Christ." **(Ephesians 5: 19-20)**

My heart is overflowing with praise and love for my wonderful Savior. This past week I have awakened with a precious chorus going through my mind. It starts like this: *"The more that I serve Him, the sweeter He grows, the longer I serve Him my heart overflows!"* I have searched for it in the hymnals that I have but have not been able to find it. This has been going on for over a week. It started when I was still struggling to get victory over some things I was going through in my life.

The other day I picked up a copy of the Herald of His coming, a Christian publication, and came upon this heading to an article, *"CHANGING A BURDEN TO A SONG."* It appeared over an article by Walter Beutlet. I am sure that he won't mind my using the title for my chapter. When I read it I said to the Lord: *"Why, that is the title for my chapter, that is what You are doing in my life!"*

Truly these days I am walking with a song in my heart. If we are sincere with our Lord and really want His way more than anything—He will turn our burdens into songs. **"Weeping may endure in the night, but joy cometh in the morning."** **(Psalm 30:5)** Are all my burdens gone? By no means. But as we realize we can roll the burdens over on Him, and only follow His direction we no longer carry the responsibility. Sometimes we hinder what He is trying to do in the lives of our loved ones by trying to tell Him how to work it out. He has something wonderful in store for them, but it must be worked out His way and His time. Our church's Homecoming begins August 20. We are in the midst of our cottage prayer meetings—seeking to get our hearts right with the Lord, so He can work through us as channels for His glory. It is amazing. As we examine our hearts before the Lord, we discover so many things that we hadn't thought of and that need to be cleansed by the blood of the Lord. The Lord first brought to my mind several people. I had been watching and noticing all the things they did wrong. Rather than see my own judgmental attitude I was seeing they needed to get right with the Lord, especially as I thought those things were done to me. I cried out to the Lord about it. He spoke to me and told me that I was to do good to those who despitefully used me and return good for evil. I set out to do just that. For awhile I saw no difference, but praise the Lord, He not only changed their attitudes but mine also. There is much to be accomplished yet, but the walls are down and peace has been restored. One thing we find out: There are several sides to the story, and God Who sees the whole picture is the only one who is capable of seeing the real answer. We long so to keep Christ on the throne of our hearts and self on the cross. Somehow it seems that self gets in the way of what Christ is trying to do.

As we are living in the last days, Satan is trying so many tricks to throw us off track. As an angel of light, he knows that we wouldn't go into temptation if the sin was obvious.

At this time he is doing every thing he can to break up the home, especially among the spiritual Christian. He can make a thing sound so spiritual that we think it must be of the Lord, while all along he is trying to tear into the very foundation of the Christian home. His main target is to attack the homes of the spiritual leaders and destroy their marriages. Because of the books I have written, I received many letters from some wonderful Christians. And you would be surprised at the tactics the devil uses. Many times when a man of God is counseling with someone, trying to help that person, they are drawn to the person. If they don't realize it, in time their whole ministry is destroyed. The same thing can happen even with a friend trying to help one who has been hurt. So we need to be on our guard. It is good for each person to visit only their own sex unless a third person is present. For example there once was a pastor who was strong for the Lord. During World War II, when gas was short motorists often would pick up hitchhikers. As this pastor followed this practice, there was a certain girl who was at the same corner every morning and the pastor would give her a ride. As they rode together, they began to be friends. He began to be drawn to her. It doesn't take a wife long to pick up on these things, and the pastor's wife began to spend much time in prayer and the Lord would always direct her when she was to go to the office. In time, the pastor came to his senses and realized what was happening. He began to change his route to the office and therefore avoided seeing the girl. He began preaching of the dangers of picking up people and warned the people to take a different route each morning. Because he realized in time what was happening, his ministry was saved, and he went on to a richer ministry in our Lord until the Lord called him home. I wrote a similar instance in my first book that only prayer brought me through—a friend of mine was going through the same thing. She let down her barriers one time, and even though the Lord forgave her, every time she would hear her husband tell everyone what a wonderful wife he had, she would mentally whip herself as she would think, *"Oh, if he only knew."*

  Satan uses different approaches from time to time. As I have said, he uses most the thought we are helping someone and instead that person is pulling us down. Satan knows that we belong to our Lord. He can't take away from us our salvation. But he can destroy our testimony and therefore keep us from leading others to the Lord.

  I have been going through a real test. It seems that my whole body has been racked with pain, especially in my arms and legs. I was helpless, I could hardly get my clothes off and on. I literally cried as I tried. I had to give up getting into a tub, as I couldn't get out and it was impossible to wait on myself, get into the car, etc. And when I needed help I had no one. So I struggled alone in pain.

My children live out of town, and when they heard of my condition they felt I needed to come live with them. At the same time the folks at church want me to teach a class this next year. I have been praying for the Lord to give me wisdom as to what He would have me do. I feel that the Lord would have me accept the class. I will be going forward in faith. Also, there were several personal problems I needed to take care of. Yesterday was a bad day. I had so much pain I even cried at times. Last night I received a letter from Lottie, a friend of mine. She told me about Lillie, another friend, who was also living alone. Her son wants her to come live with him and his wife. Lottie told her as long as she could walk from the coffee pot to the table she should stay at home. Well I can do that. Lottie has been having severe health problems, but she lives alone. Her friends and neighbors are always looking after her in various ways. Lottie was a person who always did for folks older than she; and now the people are doing for her.

Thinking on my own problem, I feel there is much to do in my church and home. I don't believe it is time to move. This morning when I was having my quiet time with the Lord, I started to do some real heart searching, to see where I stood with the Lord. There was one situation I had been praying about that I really think the Lord is working out. I believed the situation would soon be behind me. The Lord spoke to me to see if I was willing for it to be worked out in a different way, which would involve me. I came to the place where I turned it over to the Lord. After weighing the question, I knew He would do a work of grace that would allow me to go through it.

Pat Mendoza called me last night. She had gone through a time like mine and she was six months getting over it. She was going to bring down her books and equipment so I could do therapy at home. I thought about six months. Was I willing to accept that, with so much to do? Of course we don't have the say over that. It really helps when we see God's hands in it and accept it from

Him. Then we can go forward in faith knowing the Lord won't put more on us than we are able to bear. I have come to the place where I realize that His will is the only important thing there is, regardless of what it calls for. I now have peace about everything, knowing again that Romans 8:28 still holds true. This morning, while I am still sore, I am much better. I have gotten so many things accomplished. While I am still sore, it is truly a miracle-will I keep on getting better? I don't know. But I am praising the Lord for everything He is doing for me. I have learned that the only way to live a peaceful, happy, life is to give it all to Him and know that He knows far more than I do what will make me happy. I will be going to the doctor this following Tuesday. Then I will find out what is really going on. I feel that it is either arthritis or bursitis. In either case, having the Lord go with me through all of it, makes it bearable, now I am singing as I work.

I went to the doctor and he gave me medication to take. Six pills later I am so much better. If all goes well, I will not have six months to bear. Our Lord is precious. He is longsuffering and patient with us. We are in our third day in revival. The Lord is there. You can feel His presence. Only one saved so far. He was a little nine-year old boy.

Great things are taking place in our hearts. Our evangelist is Rev. William Gregory. He lives on the Eastern shore of Virginia. If you ever get a chance to sit under his ministry, you will be blessed. He is just an everyday Christian, very humble. But you are not with him very long till you feel the presence of the Holy Spirit there. We are doubly blessed, as our pastor is also a spirit-filled man. If we come to church with our hearts open for a blessing, we shall not go away unblessed.

Last night ended our revival. Each night the message was better. Thursday night the evangelist spoke on forgiveness. That is so important. One night he told us about a friend of his. A man had abused the friend's daughter who was only eleven at the time. He let hatred build up in his heart, and he became bitter. His pastor would always tell Joe (not his real name) that he had to let go of the hatred. Rev. Gregory said he had just about given up on Joe. However, just before he left to come here, Joe came to church and came forward and let go of the hatred. Rev. Gregory said he will be baptizing him when he goes home.

The next morning Rev. Gregory had gone to Hardee's for breakfast. There was the usual crowd there, most of them drank. They were old friends of Joe. Joe came in, and when they saw his face, they wanted to know what happened to him. He was so filled with joy that he had to tell them all about it, pointing to the preacher as the one the Lord used to help him see the light. They listened intently. Finally one of them said, "I'm glad for you Joe." The pastor has been trying to reach these fellows for quite a time. Will this open the door to that group? We pray that it will.

Last night he spoke from the 37th Psalm, the first 5 verses. *"Fret not thyself because of evil doers, neither be thou envious against the workers of iniquity. For they shall soon be cut down like the grass, and wither as the green herb. Trust in the Lord, and do good; so shall thou dwell in the land, and verily thou shalt be fed. Delight thyself also in the Lord; and He shall give thee the desires of thine heart. Commit thy way unto the Lord; trust also in Him; and He shall bring it to pass."* He made it so clear as he spoke on integrity and brought it down to our level. He pointed out that so many Christians fail to realize that they should be a lighthouse to the people around them. If people see them cheating on their income tax, wasting their time on the job, carrying off small items from the job, etc. unfortunately they may think they are hypocrites. These are things that people have gotten use to doing and thinking nothing about. As he spoke, he told of selling a house to his nephew. While the nephew wasn't able to buy it at the time, they made some arrangement for the nephew to rent it until he can buy it. The nephew went all out to make repairs on the place. He was so grateful to his uncle for working with him that he put all the canceled checks in an envelope and sent them to his uncle so he could take them off his taxes. Of course, the uncle knew that wouldn't be right, so he just threw them in the waste basket. That was far better than to always feel guilty about it.

It reminded me back when I was having so many hospital and medical bills. Several people wanted me to deed my land to my children, then I could apply for Medicaid and have reduced medical cost. At this time so many of the people were doing just that. Somehow I couldn't. I just didn't feel right about it. The Lord has blessed me for that. Even though I had the bills, He has gone before and I have been able to keep up. No amount of money could make up for always having a guilty feeling. His peace is worth everything. The ones who resort to doing those things come to the place where their whole life caves in. They have built their house on the sand. We may seemingly take the hard way, but our house is built on the rock and will stand forever.

Rev. Bill Gregory gave us much to think about for days to come. Pray for him and about the many burdens he carries for his people. Few people realize the burdens a man of God carries.

This should remind us to pray constantly for our pastors. Few people realize what they go through, and how prayer can lighten the load. The longer I serve Him the sweeter He grows.

I just came across something that Talmage wrote. He was a godly man. He said, *"God cares not for the length of our prayers, or the number of our prayers. It is the faith in them that tells."* As I think of this, I realize how much the Christian life is one of the heart. This is something I pray about, as I long to pray in the Lord's will. The Lord alone know the hearts of the people we are praying for. He is the only one who really knows what has to take place in that person's heart to bring him to the place of calling out to the Lord. WE MUST ALLOW HIM TO WORK IT OUT HIS WAY AND NOT TELL HIM WHAT TO DO. He is wonderful! Let's trust Him!

CHAPTER TWELVE

GOD NEVER MAKES A MISTAKE

"And we know that all things work together for good to those that love God, to them who are called according to His purpose." **(Romans 8:28)**

In looking over the last chapter, I am amazed that two months have flown by since I even looked at this book. Where does the time go! So many things have happened since then. I will try and capture it all and put it down in sequence. I had planned a prayer seminar before I had gotten sick, to be held on the 23rd of September. I decided to go forth in faith with that also. When I told Dr. Goss about it, he told me I could take an extra pill that day to see me through. Things went fine, but on my next visit to Dr. Goss, he sent me to Dr.. Giuliano, who specializes in arthritis. He would be able to prescribe the right medication for me. You learn so much and I found out there are seven kinds of arthritis. The Doctor suspected that I had P.M.R. and Giant cell arthritis. He sent me to Dr. Brewer, who is a surgeon to have him take a piece of artery out just below my temple. Praise the Lord, that proved negative. It would have involved years instead of months. Dr. Giuliano isn't sure of my arthritis, but he gave me a shot of cortisone in my left arm. For a while I couldn't use my hands at all and my shoulders were in constant pain. Thanks be to God I am much better. Our Lord is wonderful!

Recently I discovered a little book by Charles Allen on the 23rd Psalm. It is a remarkable book. The purpose of the book was to help discouraged and depressed people. He suggested that it will help anyone who follows the directions. You begin by reading the Psalm five times a day. Don't quote it. Read it slowly the first thing upon getting up. Read it again after breakfast, again at lunch, again just before the evening meal, and finally just before going to bed. Repeat this each day for a week. He promises you will be a different person at the end of the week. One fellow said, "I am so busy that I read it five times when I first get up." Rev. Allen replied, "when the doctor gives you pills, do you take them all at once?" You must take them as directed! If you ever get an opportunity to get a copy, it will be worthwhile to read it.

Time seems to pass so quickly. I got a call on the 17th telling me that my great granddaughter was in a serious car accident. She is a beautiful 17 year old young lady. The accident happened while driving to school. At the time of my writing this it will be two weeks tomorrow and she is just beginning to respond. She had many injuries also. Her arm was broken and her lung punctured. She will need some plastic surgery for areas under her chin. We lost her grandfather on Easter Monday with a massive heart attack. While we are seeing some improvement, she will have many hard days ahead. We have a merciful Lord, and He loves her even more than we do.

I firmly believe we are in the last days. So much is happening in various places with many people. It causes you to cry out, "*Even so come quickly Lord Jesus.*" What ever we are called to go through, our Lord is going through it with us, carrying the heaviest part of the load. We always should pray that our faith won't fail.

I am enjoying teaching again. We just finished studying Ezra and are starting in the book of Nehemiah. We have learned much. My Sunday School class enters into the lesson, and that makes it more interesting. I truly have to lean on the Lord, it has been so long since I taught. Except the Lord teach through me, there is little benefit to others. If we are only going to teach a history lesson we will gain much information, but it will not change our lives. We need to apply everything to our lives and find out what the Lord is trying to tell us. Then we must be obedient to Him. It is the Word of God through prayer that brings the change in our lives.

I went for a little walk the other day. It was a beautiful October day and the sun was shining. After the frost, we can see the different trees changing colors. Surprisingly enough, there are many of the trees that are still green. As I thought on these things I believe that is how our Lord works on us. We cannot change until we are fully yielded to our Lord. Many of our churches seem to go so far and then stop, afraid of what will happen if they give control of themselves to the Lord. Romans 12:1-2 says, **"Present your bodies a living sacrifice unto God, which is your reasonable service. Be not conformed to this world, but be ye transformed by the renewing of your mind, that ye may prove what is that good, and acceptable, and perfect will of God."** Yes, we will have trials and troubles enter our lives; not only to get our attention, but also to refine us that we may become more and more like Him. What a joy it is when we are willing to take up our cross daily and follow Him. He is always there and we have His peace so therefore we can press on. We never know what living is until we let Him take all of us!

I have written many things that I have endured since starting this book. My hope is, that in reading about it, you will also see intertwined through it the perfect peace that the Lord gave me. If it had not been there, the hurt would have been too great to write about. He makes the difference. Perhaps it is that loved one that has gone astray, or that precious one lying upon a bed of sickness. You may have lost your job or you are having financial problems. By reading some of the things I have experienced and am going through I pray you will be encouraged and you will know that the Lord does love and care for you. Looking to Him, He will go with you through all these trials.

When the trials are behind us we won't remember the pain even though we know it was bad, but we will remember all the little things our Lord has done for us. Faye, a friend of mine, upon reading my second book, *"Precious Memories"* said, "how can you call it *'Precious Memories'* when it is so full of suffering and trials?" Betty, another friend of mine was with us, at the time. She has suffered much sickness for several years. I turned to Faye, and said, *"One day when Betty was lying on the couch so sick, she looked over to the chair and said, 'Lord, if you were sitting there, what would you say to me?'"* She felt the nearness of His presence and He again held out to her **Isaiah 40:31,** *"They that wait upon the Lord shall renew their strength; they shall mount up with wings as eagles: they shall run and not be weary; they shall walk and not faint."* Then I asked Betty, "When you think of that time, what do you remember the most, the pain you were going through or that experience you had with the Lord?" She said, "It really did happen and I will always remember speaking to Him and how He gave me that verse again. Since then every time I get low or depressed He always allows that verse to come to me." So you see, dear ones, it is not the suffering—everybody goes through suffering, but how our Lord works it all out for His glory, if we are His and will let Him. As I write about my trials and suffering I hope you see Christ all through them. He has been so precious to me. I pray I will never turn my back on Him. He is my life, morning, noon, and night. Praise His name, He is wonderful!

One last thing —when looking through my *book shelf I happened to come across a little book called, "18 No time to waste."* It has been there for years and I doubt if I ever read it. Looking closely, I saw it was about an eighteen year-old girl who was killed in a car accident. Along with her were two boys who were also killed and a third one badly injured. They didn't expect him to live. They were coming from a mission camp and the four of them had told the Lord that whether it be by life or death they wanted His name to be glorified. Three killed and one left. The Lord used the death of these three to reach many of the young people they had witnessed to. Their death brought forth much fruit. The one the Lord chose to leave behind went through much suffering, but through his life many more turned to him to seek answers as to why some are taken and others left. The three graves drew many people to the Lord when they heard the story. The Lord's name was truly glorified. Our Lord never makes a mistake.

CHAPTER THIRTEEN

Satan Cannot Get Into The Heart Of A Grateful Christian

"Be careful for nothing: but in everything by prayer and supplication with thanksgiving let your request be known to God, and the peace of God, which passes all understanding, shall keep your hearts and minds through Christ Jesus." (Philippians 4:6-7)

    I can't believe it! Thanksgiving is almost upon us. The time passes so quickly when you are older. So much has happened since last Thanksgiving, and it is hard to take it all in. Circumstances do change things, and you find that you can't always keep the customs you always kept. Last year all the family was here, with the exception of one son who couldn't make it. I told in a previous chapter how we gathered together every year.
    My two sons in Richmond got together, and have planned to pick me up, we were going to have Thanksgiving up there this year.
    Although they always brought food, I felt that I should cook more. I was afraid that there would not be enough. You would think that I would be reluctant to give that up, but praise the Lord, I am rejoicing that the responsibility has been taken out of my hands. For several years I had prayed for the strength to go through with it. The Lord always gave me the strength, and He knew it was time to bring about a

change. I have found that when the Lord wants me to do a thing, His strength is enough to carry me through. There is a time when we need to let go and let the younger generation take over and start new traditions.

I know I will be in town for Christmas, because I have a Doctor's appointment on December 22. I just can't let that pass without doing something for my Lord. As I was working around the house this morning, a plan was formed in my mind. I believe that the Holy Spirit placed it there. At least I will walk forth in faith toward that goal. I have two granddaughters that have offered to put up my tree and bake a cake. Here is my plan: I would get a team of six teen-age girls, and we would plan a birthday party for Jesus. I would let them do most of the planning. We could invite twelve little children. As we would gather around the tree, I would tell the Christmas story. Then we would give each of the children a small gift. Have a cake, ice cream, and candies for them. Then we would play several games. Each of the girls would have two children to look after. Each team of two would be assigned to a certain job. That way there would be no confusion. I believe that the older children would receive a blessing, knowing that they had made someone's Christmas happier. For many people the holidays bring on depression. We can ask the Lord to lead us to the right people, and invite them in for a simple meal. They would go away feeling encouraged, because they knew that someone cared. We find that Satan always comes up with something to keep people's minds off the true meaning of Christmas. Many parent's are guilty of feeling their children are too young to understand the things of the Lord. They are always talking about Santa Claus and getting the children excited about something that isn't true. They have no problem with the children understanding about that. When children begin asking questions about the child Jesus, we need to put everything else aside and answer their questions honestly. God will give the understanding. I know of one little girl who was five years old, that began questioning her parents. The parents had been having family devotions, and she had been memorizing scripture, so her heart was being prepared. She kept asking questions on how to be saved. After listening for awhile, she would go upstairs. One day, she came downstairs and said, "Well, I did it! I asked Jesus to come into my heart." It wasn't long before she started to talk to her brother, who was three years old. She would tell him that he was a sinner, and that he needed to be saved. One day his grandmother was there, and she took him somewhere. As they were riding, he turned to her and asked her if she was saved.

A year later, they were all together again. He had a toy set of David and Goliath, and was playing with them. His grandmother asked him who gave them to him. He said, "Mama got them for my birthday." She said, "You know it isn't your birthday." He said, "It is too. I was born again last year." O, for the faith of a little child! Both this little boy and his sister are bold in their faith. I have a great grandson who will be four in March, who asks questions once in a while. Keeping my granddaughter alert. Sometimes he goes to his daddy. She is trying to answer him in a way he will understand. The Lord tells us, **"Except we become as little children, we cannot enter the Kingdom of God."**

Now to get back to my subject of Satan not being able to get into the heart of a grateful Christian. Remember, Satan will do everything within his power to throw you off track. When the depressing thoughts come, know where they come from. The best way that I know to resist the devil is to start making a list of all the blessings that the Lord has given you. Also look beyond the pain and heartache, and know our Lord has given His promise that all these things will work together for our good. I see so many ways that this year has worked for my good. Our Heavenly Father has brought much good through the death of my son, and through the healing of his granddaughter. She wrecked her car and was in a coma for several weeks. Praise the Lord she has come out of it now, and recognizes the different ones around her. I believe the Lord is using this to bring healing to many people. All around us, we see people going through so many terrible things and say, "What is good about that?" We can pray earnestly for them and that their suffering will not be in vain, but will lead them to Jesus.

Oh, what a joy that will be. ***"Even the angels in heaven will rejoice,"*** and the ones involved will feel as though a hundred-ton weight has been lifted from their backs. ***"as far as the east is from the west, so far has He removed our transgressions from us."*** **Psalm 103:12**

    The suffering and confusion that I have been going through has helped me to be more sensitive to the suffering of others. It has taken away the doubts in my mind when I see a brother who seems to be confused. Praise the Lord for He is good. May praise and thanksgiving ever be His.

    So, let's sit down and start writing out our blessings. Have plenty of paper handy. You will find out you have so many blessings you could never be discouraged.

    This past week-end the Lord gave me the privilege of going to Claremont Baptist Church in Claremont, VA. I was given the Sunday School hour and ten minutes in the worship service. What a joy to be able to share with these dear folks, and tell them the things the Lord is doing in my life. It humbles me to tell about it. I realize once again, how much the Lord has done for me. He is the Almighty God, and yet He takes time with me. He has brought me to the place where I cannot love Him enough. If He would do all that for me, just think what He can and will do in your life, if you will let Him. Sometimes I can't seem to express in words all that I want to tell Him. Praise the Lord, the Holy Spirit sees the things in my life that will hinder me, and convicts me of them, so that I can make those things right. Oh yes, the little church gave me a hundred and five dollar donation to help with the publication of my books. Our Lord is good. Let's praise His name.

    I want you to notice the scripture at the beginning of the chapter. Our Lord says that we are not to worry. We are to pray and ask humbly with <u>thanksgiving</u>, and if we do that, He promises that He will give us that peace. A peace that passeth all understanding. Praise His name, when we have that peace we can face anything. Therefore is the Lord's name glorified. Those who are not Christians cannot understand it. While we don't see the answer, we are assured that it is on the way.

One day I received a letter from Dr. Henry, giving me the name and address of Dot Winfield. He asked me to write her, and to pray for her son Phillip. He was on drugs, and it was breaking his mother's heart. Through the years that we corresponded I came to know her in a special way. Few mothers would have gone through what she was put through, and love enough to keep on praying for him. She also carried out each thing she felt the Lord wanted her to do. The Lord blessed her and she has seen that prayer answered in a wonderful way. I was especially touched when I read her son's testimony. He told how one day, when he came back from his last fling, Dot met him at the door, and lovingly said, "This one was a hard one, wasn't it son?" No wonder her prayers were answered. Most of us would have stood at the door ranting and raving.

Dot helped me with my second book. I will always count her as a special friend.

Testimony of Philip Winfield

I thank God for growing up in a Christian home. There were so many years I spent away from the Lord. I always knew that returning to the Lord would make the difference that I was missing in my life.

I started using alcohol when I was fourteen years old, getting drunk and getting sick was how it started. The alcohol seemed to make me feel so good and I liked it anyway. As I look back now I see how my sin progressed over the years, starting with that first drink. Then I started smoking pot, which was one of the things I said I would never do. I didn't like it at first, but after a while I got used to it and loved it. At the age of sixteen or seventeen we were smoking it all the time, before school, during school and after school. We could hardly do anything without it. Then we started with pills, speed and acid. We would do almost anything to get high. I started dropping out of school activities. I didn't want to be involved with any of that, because drugs were more important.

I graduated from high school with a "D" average. I

barely made it. I started experimenting with Cocaine about that time, but it was very expensive so I did not do it much. Over the next several years I kept drinking heavy and smoking pot heavy. In 1986 I had an accident, and received a D. W. I. and to this day I still don't remember the accident. I was in the hospital for 17 days. I dislocated my hip, got 30 stitches in my face and got a big gash in my shoulder. I had to have plastic surgery on my face and shoulder and years later when I was only 28 I had to have my hip replaced. That was a scary time for me. I remember feeling so alone, but now I know that the Lord was with me all the time. I stopped using drugs and drinking for about a year as a result of the accident, but started back up again and things got worse. I started smoking pot and drinking again after one of my hip operations. At that time that was what I thought I was missing. As the years went by my drug use increased to the point of losing my job and self esteem.

    I remember from time to time going to church with mom. When the services reached toward the end and they would give the invitation, I had to hold on to the pew with both hands because I knew the way I was living was not right. The tears would start to come but I forced myself not to lose it. They would always play *"I Surrender All"* every time I went, no matter when I went they played that song, it used to tare me up inside. Just writing about it now makes me cry, but that's okay I'm not afraid to show emotion today (Thank God). I did not go to church very often but those times I did stuck with me. When the end of the service was finally over I would say to myself *"Whew I made it through another service"*. A year later I was deeper and deeper into drug addiction. As a result of my accident in 1986 I received a larger settlement which blew open my drug use. It got to the point that I was using about $500.00 a day of cocaine. I had lost 45 pounds and a lot of respect and more self esteem. I could go on and on about those times but all of them together was finding more drugs, etc. I lost three jobs, wrecked three cars and was operated on about 6 times as a result of being addicted to drugs. If I had to do it all over again I wouldn't change one thing because it took me right where I needed to be. It took me to the cross where Jesus died for my sins. Even through all I did to ruin my life, Jesus still loves me, more than I can imagine. I'll never forget the last day I used drugs. It was April 13, 1993, I was supposed to work that weekend, but did not show up or even call in. My parents did not know where I was. I would always leave and would not come back for days. It was a Sunday morning about 9 o'clock. I will never forget that ride home. When I got there Mom was waiting for me crying as I came in. She said to me this has been a tough one, hasn't it? At that point I did not know what to say. I was really at the bottom of my life. We talked about going into drug treatment and I think I was really ready this time. I went downstairs and I started to cry and I could not stop. As I laid on the couch crying, in my mind a picture of Christ with His arms stretched out to me kept flashing to me. At that point I felt a peace come over me and I knew it was going to be all right. I prayed for help, Christ heard my prayers and on that day, April 18th, they were answered. I went in for treatment for 14 days and learned a lot about myself and praise God I have been clean ever since. When I was in for treatment the pastor from White Marsh Baptist Church came to visit me. I told him I wanted to give my life to Christ and be re-baptized. He gave me a book call **GOOD NEWS AMERICAN, GOD LOVES YOU**. In the back of the book was the sinner's prayer. I went back to my room, got on my knees and said the prayer and again I felt a peace come over me. When I got out of the treatment center I went to the White Marsh Baptist Church and made a public profession of my life. This time I was ready to make that walk down the aisle, my heart was beating like a bass drum. I was baptized several weeks later.

    I cannot say enough for what Christ has done for me. He has done it all!! I never thought my life would be this full and abundant. I thank God for loving the world so much that He sent His only Son to die for a sinner like me. Jesus Christ is the only way.

CHAPTER FOURTEEN

OUR GOD IS SOVEREIGN

"But as for you, ye thought evil against me; but God meant it unto good." (Genesis 50:20)

The Lord has been bringing so many people into my life that have been unjustly accused of things that they are not guilty of.

One week-end my granddaughter and her husband brought home a hitch-hiker they picked up. We kept him over night, and as we talked I was able to catch some of his story. He was walking with a Christian group that loved the Lord, his brother had him put away because he said that he was losing his mind. The young fellow had escaped and had started out to get as far away as he could from that state. He had nothing but the clothes on his back. We washed them and gave him something to put on. I also gave him a New Testament plus one of my books. As I talked to him I could see that he really loved the Lord and was going to serve Him no matter what. I truly believe his story. After our talk he went upstairs to get some rest. Shortly after that my doorbell rang, I answered it and there stood a young fellow at the door. Someone had given him one of my books to read, and he knew God wanted him to meet me. Neil, a very likable young man, wanted to talk to me, so we went into my office, and that began a long friendship. Neil was facing severe problems from his wife taking him to court and falsely accusing him. These charges were totally untrue.

She has found another man, and at one point she told him that she would never divorce him, but before she got through with him he would wish she had. She said, "I am going to bury you alive." Being new to this area and attending different churches they had not yet settled in any of them. The wife who found a good job, also acquired a boy friend, and began to push Neil out. He had only gotten several part time jobs at this time. Later God led in introducing him to a local pastor and he began attending his church. Sometimes he felt that if only they had found this church sooner things would not have taken the turn that it did. He was and is burdened with lost souls and soon his pastor also caught that vision.

Neil was given notice that he was to appear in court on a certain Thursday. I didn't see him for awhile. About a week later he came to my home. When I asked him where he had been he told me he had just gotten out of jail. I couldn't believe it! I asked him to tell me how it happened. This is the story I got. His wife was there with her new boyfriend and she was before the judge. She told the judge that he had stalked her and her children the night before all the way to Lynchburg. He was so amazed, he cried out in court that she was a liar. He told them to check with his pastor as he was at prayer meeting and choir practice that night until 9:00. The judge said, "Are you calling her a liar?" Neil said, "Yes Sir, I am." The judge turned to the sheriff and said, "Lock him up." So he was taken to jail. He spent a week there and he told me it was just like Joseph in the Bible as the Lord had given him favor not only with the sheriff and the deputies, but with the prisoners as well. Not knowing what to expect he had taken his Bible, my book, his walkman and quite a few Christian tapes. As the inmates watched him that week they saw his love for the Lord, and realized the Lord's hand was upon him.

After a week they released him on his word that he would come back when it came up in court. He gave his word and the prisoners all helped him to pack. They asked him to remember them which he promised them he would do. Many of them asked how he could be so peaceful at a time like that when he didn't even smoke. He shared a little about Christ with them, and what he had done in his life. He also shared some of his books, and promised to get them copies of my book. I gave him quite a few and he took them back to the prisoners. With the exception of one or two, the people were all so kind. The Lord used this week to establish his testimony among the people.

    Four months later at the trial, his wife accused him of molesting her daughter by a deceased husband. He loved her children so much it deeply hurt him. To make things worse she accused him of doing the same with other children where he was a former teacher at a Christian school. The mother took the girl to social workers and she and social workers convinced the child the accusation was true. His daughter was a sweet little girl and kept her head down and voice lowered during the questioning. Neil had always romped with the children and they had a good time together. But something like that was never in his mind. He was never accused of the act but of improper advances. The judge again said, "Guilty". The sheriff came and took him although he didn't even put handcuffs on him. I want to read verbatim what Neil wrote that day, "All my anxiety is gone. There is no more bleeding, no ulcers, and no pain. The acid in my stomach seems fine. Once I heard the sheriff was taking me total peace returned." The sheriff said, "I hope they are happy now." Neil thanked me for praying for him. At first he thought the men were all stand-offish because of the charges against him. I received a letter later that said, "They have all accepted me. It has been neat to watch the change. I get no mockery for reading my Bible or if I pray for my food or for not swearing or smoking.

    Still there are times when he felt pretty low. Just before he was to receive his sentence he wrote, "It's not much longer until the 16th. Please pray that the judge will let me out. However, I am very much willing to do as God pleases just as your letter stated. I don't mind being here if that's what the Lord wants, but I really feel so hindered in my ministry. It is so hard to pray. It is never quiet. I get so tired of the T. V. I told my pastor yesterday if I get to thinking it's really bad. I try to think what prison must have been like for Paul or John Bunyun. I guess they would look at this like it was a Holiday Inn."

"I do find it difficult finding quiet time. There is no place to go. The phone rings at the guards station constantly. The TV. is always blaring and the foul mouths are always yelling over that. My only peace is between 3 and 5 A.M. before breakfast is brought at 6 and we are unlocked from our individual cells. It makes it hard to read and get something out of it. I just hope it isn't very much time in here and I'm out. Please pray because I'm afraid they are going to give me a lot of time." These are taken from various letters he has written to me from time to time. There is so much more I would like to share but I will leave it at that.

Now we will turn to the good things about this. Since being there he has won all the prisoners to Christ except two. One of them left with a Bible and had been told the way plainly. The other one heard the gospel also.

When visiting the jail this past week only 5 prisoners beside himself were there. All are now Christians and are involved in Bible study. He has heard the voice of the Lord telling him that this is his mission field for the six months. He said to me, "The Lord must have shown you before He showed me because you were always talking about my ministry, and sharing in it.

I cannot close this without telling you about one special guard. We will call her Mary. She is a deep Christian and so good to all the prisoners. Neil told me that he thanked God daily for placing her to be their guard. She will even enter into prayer and Bible Study with him, his visitors and the inmates. She is not only kind to him but to all the prisoners. The Lord will bless her for her ministry of kindness to them. While all the guards were good, she went the second mile with them, because bars can't keep out communion of His children.

I have started teaching the book of Esther in my Sunday school class. While the name of God is not mentioned in the entire book we have a picture of God placing the right people in the right places to accomplish His plans. I see Him doing this with Neil, his pastor and my life.

He is working through them to harvest a great field of

souls to Himself before He returns. Oh, that all of us would be so yielded to Him that He could place us into the field He has for us to harvest. The sooner we are all in place, the sooner the Lord can reap a harvest of souls through us, and hasten His return. My pastor says we need to get ready so when this work begins we are ready to take our places; the sooner the return of our precious Lord! Are we holding back the work of God? Or are we helping it to go forth and hasten His coming?

The following story was written about Neil. He used another name but it was about his Christmas Eve right after all this started to happen. I will follow this story and tell you about this Christmas.

VISION OF LONELINESS

Ten numbers, "Yes dial them stupid," his mind prodded.

He stared at the phone and felt a stab to dial a second time, but pride stifled the urge. He glanced around the single room, he reviewed its few possessions. There was a double bed neatly made by the housekeepers, a bare round table in front of the single window, a television on a shelf in the corner, and a built-in dresser to hold belongings. A single chair with wooden arms filled another corner near the phone.

For the third time the thought plagued his mind. But as before, he forced the longing temporarily to the corners of his mind.

Chad threw his body on the maroon comforter, and let his mind go. The vision played clearly before his closed eyes.

There she was frantically skipping from one pan to the other. It was Mom, she was dressed, befitting of the pastor's wife, in a bright red dress protected by her favorite Christmas apron.

Chad opened his eyes, and realized the smell of home cooked mashed potatoes, green beans, and simmering gravy was only imaginary.

"Should he pick up the phone and interrupt the joyous

occasion?" He closed his eyes again and saw a man smiling broadly. Dad leaned over and picked up a festively dressed granddaughter. She giggled as he lifted her to the ceiling and kissed her on the descent. Her laughter only added to the noise of the other eleven grandkids who were running around with excitement. Grandpa shooed them away from the mounds of brightly wrapped packages spilling from under a twinkling Christmas tree.

The pain in his heart opened his watery eyes only to see the spackled ceiling. Chad blinked back the tears as he staggered to the window. He pulled back the institutional matching drape and viewed the wet pavement and mist on the parking lot.

"Not many cars tonight," he thought. "Who would be in a motel on Christmas Eve?" he answered himself.

Would Dad want to hear my voice tonight? Or would he start crying and ruin the entire evening with sadness?"

He returned to his bed and the projected images bounced before his eyes again.

Paper, ribbons and bows flew everywhere as the children all shouted at once over their sought for gifts.

"It's beautiful grandma! Thank you so much."

"That's exactly what I wanted!"

Missing from the scene were Chad and his family. He turned over, tore back the comforter and smothered his head in the pillow to cry. He had driven past a living Nativity, watched a Christmas Eve service on T.V., and read his Bible. Nothing helped or changed the fact that he was alone on this Holy night.

Reaching the end of his tears, he glanced at his watch. He wasn't in very good shape to attend the local church service at 11:00 p.m.

"Maybe I shouldn't go. They'll wonder why I am alone and ask me questions."

He thought about staying in the motel room, but as he looked around he realized there was no Christmas there. He washed his red eyes and dressed in fresh clothes.

A crisp, damp breeze ate to his bones as he jumped into the car. A moment later he looked at a packed church parking lot and felt the need to run, but a still small voice pushed him on and he located a place to park.

Chad's heart beat faster as he approached the church. He took in a deep breath of the cool air, grasped the handle and pulled to open the oversized door.

To his surprise, candles flickered everywhere, the pews, windows, communion table, piano, organ and pulpit all donned a glowing candle. Chad paused as he drank in the strains of a familiar carol. He slowly walked down the aisle and found one partially filled pew in the packed church. Others slid down the bench as he found his place among them.

With only the movement of his eyes he searched the audience to hunt any form of familiarity, but found none. The choir sang exaltations to the King of Kings, musicians piped, *O Come All Ye Faithful*, and the congregation sang *Silent Night* as individual candles were lit one by one until a mighty light shown throughout the church.

Yet in the midst of all the excitement of music and joy, the solemn through haunted his mind. . .alone. Separation from his wife, parents, siblings, and children were almost unbearable.

And then a simple song was sung that left a repeating phrase in Chad's mind.

"Heaven must have missed you when the Father kissed you goodbye."

Chad thought, I wonder if God Almighty cried when He sent His only Son to earth to die?"

Tears sprang into his eyes again, but this time it wasn't for himself. Chad realized as never before, the love of God. Although he was alone, Jesus was his Savior. The celebration this Christmas wasn't over gifts or cards, of which he received none. It was over the true meaning of Christmas. Christ became a man in the form of a baby and that baby in the manger became his suffering Savior on a cross.

Chad climbed into bed in the motel room and spoke in an audible voice, "Thank you, Jesus, for letting me be alone so I could feel your heart." He closed his eyes and slept in peace.

Neil will soon be getting out. He, like any of us has those inward battles from time to time, but he stayed true to the Lord. Even as the Lord sent Jesus down to earth to live among us, He sent Neil there to live among them. There are several preachers that go up there each Sunday. They have been faithful to give the Word. When Neil was sent there they saw the Word lived out among them—and as each one accepted the Lord the others would see a change in them. That opened their hearts and Neil was able to share the gospel with them.

The jail is a small county jail. Rarely is there a large crowd for any length of time. Many of them are only there for less than a week.

While Neil was not able to reach them all he was able to talk to each one about the plan of salvation. The ones who left without accepting the Lord, still respected Neil and left with plans of meeting him when he got out. Hopefully the seed will bear fruit.

Christmas! Since Neil has been there, people are continually sending or bringing things to him. He in turn shares them with the inmates as they have a need. There are two outstanding times I want to write about. First, Neil had a birthday, one of the preachers brought in pizza and the inmates put their money together and got some more refreshments. The best thing was a card he got from the inmates written on ordinary paper. They all signed it. They thanked him for being a friend and for Bible study, advice, laughter, smiles, and faith. That night he said, "Thank you Lord" and turned over and wept. Second, was Christmas. So many packages and goodies came in and was shared by all. Truly we have a wonderful Lord! The greatest blessing is being in the center of the will of the Lord. This six months the jail was his mission field. Pray for Neil as he gets out, he will see clearly what the Lord wants him to do next. His sincere will is to be in the Lord's will, regardless of where that may be.

The Lord has a plan for each life. What about you? Have you given your life to the Lord completely? When I was first saved, I was told that if I wanted to be happy I would have to give my whole life to Him. They said, "before you were born-again you had a chance of some happiness, as you belonged to the devil so he would leave you alone. Now that you belong to the Lord, while Satan can never take away your salvation, he will do all he can to keep you for being fully yielded to the Lord. He doesn't want you to reach out for other souls."

When we love the Lord, Satan usually doesn't tempt us with the bigger sins as much as what we call the smaller sins. Like resentment and bitterness. If we don't watch out they can creep in before we know it. Pray for Neil, for God's direction in his life.

I, too, have used fictitious names in telling this story.

CHAPTER FIFTEEN

If You are God's Child It Does Make A Difference

"Being Confident of this very thing, that He which hath begun a good work in you will perform it until the day of Jesus Christ."
(Philippians 1:6)

    Thank you, Lord. You will not quit working with me as long as I am on this earth. This was a note that I had written in the margin of my Bible beside the above verse. I am so grateful that He doesn't leave us alone. As we go through experiences from time to time, He can show us how we have grown in Him, or our lack of growth.
    I head someone say, "If you want to know if you are a real Christian, watch your reactions when the clothesline breaks, and all your white clothes fall into the mud." I had that happen to me one day and I found myself saying, "Thank you, Lord." I knew then that God was changing my life.
    Every once in a while the Lord gives us a refresher course. It isn't that we don't know, but from time to time we need to see Him at work in our lives again. Such was the case this morning. I awoke around 4:00 A.M. My hands were hurting so badly that I decided to get up and run hot water over them to relieve the pain. In going into the kitchen I found myself walking in water. The night before as I was feeling badly, I put my dishes in the sink, covering them with water. In turning off the faucet I apparently didn't use enough pressure allowing a small amount of water to continue to run. A marvelous thing happened, I was not upset at all, but had perfect peace as I worked to get the

water up. First, I got all my towels out and put them one by one to soak up the water. I wasn't getting anywhere that way as I couldn't wring them out dry enough to take more water. Looking to the Lord, He laid on my heart to put them into the washing machine then the dryer. He gave me strength to lift them. Around 6:00 A.M. I had it pretty much under control, with the exception of cleaning up. This experience triggered my thinking of all the times He has done miracles like that for me. He is precious!

Remember our Birthday party for Jesus? Instead of having 6 teenagers we only had three. Nicole, Stephanie, (my granddaughters) and Kim (Louise's daughter). During the time of planning, Satan tried to stop it in various ways. But through it all we were determined to go ahead with it. The girls put up and decorated the tree, and also the front porch. One of the girls made the invitations while home sick. Sometimes only one could come but they all worked faithfully. They not only fixed the refreshments, but donated most of them out of their own pockets. Instead of me giving the Christmas story. Pat Mendoza, whom you will be reading about later in the book, not only gave the Christmas story, but also told us about her work in Uganda. When we knew she was coming, we opened the party to the adults as well. While we had a nice crowd, due to a snow storm many that were invited couldn't make it. The girls served refreshments first, then settled the children down to listen to the Christmas story. Several of the older children read some scriptures for her, while the others listened. After the story was told, the children all marched up to the tree for a small gift. Nicole lit the Birthday cake and the girls brought it in and all sang Happy Birthday to Jesus. Everyone commended the girls for the wonderful job they did. Pray for the three girls. Through it all I sensed that the Lord has a special ministry for them, and Satan is trying every way to block it. He doesn't want them fitting into the plan of God. After the party the girls went about putting things in order before leaving. The girls and I have been talking about starting a Bible study on Thursdays. It will be wonderful if we can.

In spite of all the big talk about wanting to turn all the

responsibilities over to the younger generation, I find I am not so willing to do that. While we had a wonderful time at my son's house Thanksgiving I think that all of them, including myself want it here Christmas. When they come to my house I keep Christmas week open as younger mothers want to have their own Christmas at home with their children. Most of them arrive sometime during that week. I miss the ones that live so far away they can't make it. Your children will always remain your children regardless of their ages. When they can't visit they always call.

Angie is coming from Florida, she will arrive on the twenty-fourth and stay until the third. While she will spend most of the time with Brenda, her mother, and her sisters, Stephanie and Nicole, she will visit with me also. (This is not the granddaughter who had the accident). The joy comes from being together as a family, not the gifts.

Around five o'clock Christmas Eve Brenda, and the three girls Angie, Stephanie, and Nicole arrived. After dinner we gathered around the tree and exchanged gifts, then we all went to their church. They were having Candle Light service. Christmas day they went to see their grandparents in Richmond. A week later the three girls called and told me they were coming for the night. The next morning we all got up and went to Sunday school. After Sunday school, we were in the sanctuary waiting for the worship service to begin, I looked up and Brenda had slipped in and was sitting with us. What a joy it was to have them. The following Monday Angie took me to the grocery store and I took advantage of this opportunity to stock up on groceries. On Tuesday my grandson Eric, came through on his way to Washington. While he had planned to go back the next day, it was two weeks later before he left. The following day he took me to the doctor. From there we went to get my medicine and several other things that I needed.

He decided to stay another day so we could have the girls over for dinner before Angie left. Angie had just left on a plane when the snow started. When we looked out the window the next morning we couldn't believe our eyes it was snowing hard and the ground was covered. I heard a knock on our door. There stood my neighbor, Louise. She had walked up to bring me a dozen eggs and two loaves of bread. About that time my son, Mark, pulled in the driveway 100 miles from Richmond. Later, looking out the window I saw Louise's husband, Ronnie, pushing snow off my driveway. What a wonderful Lord we have! I had not even prayed about any of this. My Lord just laid it on the hearts of others to think of me. My pastor also called me. He thought I was alone and wanted to have me stay at their home until the storm was over. No one expected the blizzard to last so long. Louise's son, Jeff, plowed my road on two different occasions. I am sure that the blizzard of 96 will long be remembered by everyone. The official report around here was 28 inches but in many places it was at least 33 inches.

Eric finally headed for home Monday and I am alone again. But we know we are never alone when we know the Lord!

All through this I could see the Lord's hand looking after His own. I would never be afraid to stay alone. Our Lord knows our needs even before we know them.

One of the most wonderful gifts I received this Christmas was seeing the change in Angie. She is turning back to the Lord and the change in her life is unbelievable. She has such peace in her heart and you can see the calmness and love reflected in her face. It was a joy to be around her. To think this was the same girl that said she would never come back home.

Angie left for the Air Force Reserve on the seventeenth. After her basic training she is going to school to become a dental assistant. She would return sometime in May.

Don't lose heart, those of you who have a son or a daughter who has drifted away from the Lord. ***"Nothing is impossible with the Lord."*** Angie's mother said, "When you just about give up all hope, it happens." We give all glory to the Lord!

Ridgley, a friend of mine scheduled a speaking engagement for Pat Mendoza. She was to speak to the home schoolers at the Nelson Memorial Library. The weather wasn't the best but eight mothers and thirty-five children showed up. Ridgley was putting out the African food she had prepared for Pat, when we received a phone call telling us that Pat's car had broken down. Unless the man could get it started she couldn't speak. I am anxious to find out what happened. Whatever it is I am sure the Lord will use it to further her training.

Sherri, a friend of Ridgley's was helping her to put out the food. In picking up a mango, she made the remark that a mango saved her life one day when she was on a mission trip to Africa. She had gone out under YWAM. (I had visited a chapter of that organization while in Germany. Their headquarters was an old castle. I believe they are either Pentecostal or Church of God. I have heard Loren Cunningham mention this mission work).

Ridgley had her tell the story to the children. They enjoyed it and are now anxious to hear Pat Mendoza.

Pat had been to Uganda for two months this summer. She has graciously given me an account of her days over there. While there she felt a call to go back. She leaves on the twenty-fifth of January 1996 to go to the Child Evangelism camp for six months training before going out by faith to be one of their directors there. She will need six months training also to learn the culture and as much of the language as possible. Pray for her.

Pat called me to tell me about her car. First, as she woke up that morning she reminded the Lord that she was leaving the next day and had not sold her car. She thanked Him that she still could use it to go to the meeting. (It was an old car, and she had been praying that it would hold out until she had to leave.) When she drove in to get gas it stopped and they could not get it started no matter what they tried. There she was faced with a wrecker bill and no where to haul the car to. When the man offered to buy it, she was more than glad to let him have it. She felt that was the way the Lord wanted it. She was praising the Lord for removing the last obstacle in the way. Our Lord supplied the speaker and also worked out what Pat needed to have worked out. He always works on both ends.

CHAPTER SIXTEEN

What God Was Able To Do Through One Woman That Was Open To His Word

"Let us make a little chamber, I pray thee, on the wall; and let us set for him there a bed, and a table, and a stool, and a candlestick: And it shall be, when he cometh to us, that he shall turn in thither. (II Kings 4:10)

Only one life twill soon be past!
Only what's done for Christ will last.

Can one life make a difference? Let me tell you the story of a precious friend and you be the judge. This is the story of Marjory Hatter. If you remember, I had two poems she wrote, about preacher Billy in my last book. Let me tell you a little more about her.

While she was not saved something in her heart wanted to know about the Lord. So she began to pray that the Lord would send a man to her neighborhood to preach to them and explain the Word of God. One day the Lord did send a man by the name of Billy. He stayed and a small church was formed. I am not sure if it was the present building or not. Under his preaching and teaching she was saved, she grew by leaps and bounds. Billy wasn't there very long until the Lord called him home. But not until he had laid a firm foundation among the people.

I met Marjory through Pat Mendoza. She took me down there and we had a Bible class in the fellowship hall. Marjory was always quoting what preacher Billy had taught her. At the time I met her, she was in bad health, and her husband, a fine Christian, was also in bad health.

One day she told him that the Lord had done so much for them they needed to do something in return. They owned the old homestead that he grew up in. Without much fanfare they started to fix it up. He died and I lost track of her. I prayed much about her health. One day Blanche, a friend of mine, showed me a little country newspaper. Marjory's picture was in it, she looked much better. In that same paper was a picture of their old homeplace, she had renovated it, rented out the upstairs and the downstairs was turned into a lovely "prophets chamber." All of this came about because one person cared enough to pray. She didn't quit praying and the Lord in answer to her prayer touched the hearts of Pat Mendoza, Mary and Jerry Hopkins. That is the little church in Tyro, VA, that Pat was called to do mission work in for a time. Jerry and his wife, Mary, have a wonderful ministry there. They have just completed 5 years there and the church is growing. All the people that I have met there are so friendly and you can feel the warmth of their love. A close knit fellowship. As I said, the Lord called Pat away to another ministry getting her ready to answer the call to go to the mission field. I will let Pat tell the rest of her story. I am sure her work there prepared her for what the Lord had waiting for her down the road. And in a sense, Marjory will have a part in that also. I know she will be faithful in praying for her. What is it that man says? *"No man is an island to himself."*

I will turn the rest of this over to Pat to tell her story.

PAT MENDOZA'S TESTIMONY

Christmas 1994 had it's usual and traditional fanfare for my daughter and I; get up early, pour a cup of coffee, and sit down by the tree. The traditional music floated through the air as we opened our presents.

This Christmas, however, was different for me. It was going to be my last year with my daughter. Her long awaited wedding was up coming early in spring, and I realized I would be alone with new challenges next year at this time reevaluating my life once as a single mom now as a single aging woman.

God had already started tugging at my heart, and because of my busy life as a Sunday School teacher, nursing home recreation director, and mom, I had not taken the time to seek His prodding. I also suspected the Lord wanted me to accomplish a difficult task, and my soul was being prepared to leave my comfort zone.

My daughter and I had been invited to Christmas dinner at the future in-laws, but I decided to decline the invitation, and use the day to seek the Lord's direction.

While driving to a secluded lake that Christmas morning, I began confessing my sin of coldness of heart and cried out to my precious Savior, *"Lord, I want to be completely surrendered. I no longer desire to serve my own agendas. Remove me from my comfort zone and if you will Father, use me to encourage those who need to walk closer, and to lead the lost to your glorious light."*

Walking closer to the lake, it occurred to me I was possibly putting myself in an unsafe situation. I meditated on the Lord realizing He is always with me even in an unsafe situation. His presence was so comforting, but also added to that comfort was a great big friendly dog that appeared from nowhere. He was my fleshly companion the entire day at the lake. How safe I felt in God's protection, and that of a big slobbery dog.

What did I hear from God that day? I was soon going to be free to serve in another land. I was involved in several foreign missions and perhaps I could link with them— Russia was an option as was Mexico and England. Nothing happened in my spirit which didn't necessarily mean anything, because I knew in my heart and soul the Lord was saying *"You leave your comfort zone and I will use you in another land."*

He had been preparing me for twenty plus years of my Christian walk as a struggling single parent of two children. I always knew I would work in a mission type work, and had experienced some of it working with a new little country church in Tyro, VA. I had always thought my calling would be to Mexico if I went at all due to the fact I had vacationed with my Hispanic husband, loved Mexican food, and knew a few Spanish words. However God had something else in mind. He gave me Habakkuk 2:2-4 and I went home with it.

Three days later I received a news letter from Russ Carr with Sports Outreach. As I read the letter with blurry eyes I could see the picture of Russ surrounded by lots and lots of children. I knew this was God's answer. He was speaking to my heart about the children of Africa. Africa! I'd never given that dark continent a thought. That was very foreign. Yet I knew that was it. Those African children I pictured needed someone to share Christ with them.

Russ Carr and his family lived 20 miles from me. He had been going to Africa with his sports outreach for almost 10 years taking teams from the U. S. with him. They would conduct ball clinics and then present the gospel afterwards. The children in Africa were always at the clinics but did not participate.

I called Russ right after I received his news letter and asked if he would consider taking me along when he went again. He shared with me he had never taken a woman on his short term trips, but if I could raise the support for the July trip he would take me. It ended up four of us ladies went on the trip. Russ's wife, his daughter, Lois Porter, a nurse, and myself

I have always lived on a very small budget so the thought of raising $3400 seemed impossible. *"Lord, if this is your call please give me a sign before I start such a big undertaking."* The following Sunday I shared with my Sunday School assistant what the Lord was doing in my life. I almost fainted when Nancy pledged a large sum toward this calling. *Lord, if that was your conformation and sign I thank You."* I am not sure how it happened for sure but within six months I had my needs met to go to Africa.

God not only prepared me financially but spiritually I saw how He had prepared me. After much prayer and lots of support we were ready to go.

Was I afraid? No, and I don't know why. I was more curious to what was ahead and what God was going to do. Lois and I both had prepared ourselves for the worse of conditions including wearing boots because of the *"foot parasites,"* a scarf to wear around our faces, a mosquito net, and dry shampoo due to lack of water. We had visions of bugs jumping on us. I did appreciate the suggestion to keep a journal. It is from the journal I am able to share my story.

Our flight was long with layovers in Dallas, London, and Muscat. By the time we arrived in Entelee we felt we had already been on the mission field. With twelve of us altogether we were learning lessons in servanthood, patience, and selflessness.

Barnabas, a national, who was Russ's African arm for S. O. greeted us at the airport. His smile was contagious, his warmth and humbleness made us feel very welcome to a strange country and strange sights, smells and sounds.

What a surprise when we were taken to Kampala Guest House to stay off and on for the next two weeks. It wasn't too much suffering for the Lord. We had running water, good food, soft bed. What luxury compared to what we had planned to endure.

After our arrival, washing our faces a little and changing clothes we headed for our first involvement in ministry. As we drove up to a handicapped school, we were greeted with what we found was typical of most children's homes we visited. That was smiles and friendly waves.

"Oh Lord, already I see they are so precious."

These children were even more so for most of them could not walk. They would crawl, hop, or propel rickety wheel chairs. How precious they looked in their pink uniforms. The children had baked *"cakes"* in their new outdoor oven to serve during *"tea time"*. They were so proud to have us visit them. In the humble dining room one young girl stood and thanked us for coming all the way from America to visit them. In the assembly room my heart was blessed by their simple worship, service and their love for the Lord.

God says, *":I beseech you (Pat) that you present your body a living sacrifice—be transformed by the renewing of your mind—this will prove the good, and acceptable, and perfect will of God.*

My journey, the next three weeks was mostly to learn to die to my feelings, comforts, and desires. And be made alive by Christ's wonderful power, this renewing of my mind.

How precious His Word is. The next morning we left for New Hope Orphanage where about 300 children "mobbed" our arrival. All wore nice clean uniforms they had made and the biggest smiles. The orphanage is run by Jay and Vicki Dannagles. They teach the children to be self-sufficient. They raise their own vegetables and livestock. They also try to teach a trade.

We sang and shared the gospel with these children, with many receiving Christ. Afterward, Lois Porter and I went with an older missionary lady to tour a *"fine"* hospital.

Oh Lord, please don't let me go to one of these, if I get hurt or become ill." The windows have windows with no glass, dirty mattresses, and mats on the floor for the family to sleep on and take care of the patient. The family also cooks out doors for their loved ones. After viewing the I.V s, blood unscreened, operating rooms, and sterilization techniques I decided they went to the hospital to die—period. If anyone survived in a hospital stay, it was a miracle.

We saw numbers of Aids patients and children with Malaria, parasites, and burns. The burns come from the open fire in their huts used for cooking, light and warmth.

"Such a full day, Lord, my head is swimming with all the sites, smells and sounds."

Coming back to the guest house where we were staying in Kampala, I began to realize I had seen this on TV.. It was as if it wasn't real—here it was, masses of human suffering—precious people who seemed to be lumped in one. They had no single identity to the average tourist, but I prayed, *Oh God—let me see them as you do—one individual at a time, loved by you."*

Putting my head on my pillow that night was the easy part but my sleep was disturbed by the sight of so many children!

We had seen nothing yet for soon we left for Rwanda. Armed teen-age guards stopped us arbitrarily flashing guns.

They looked like they came from the movie Rambo. They ordered us to take all our luggage down, open them, and pull all our belongings out of them. It was first humbling because these are youngsters that should have been playing cowboys and Indians, but secondly they would mock us knowing that we were at their mercy. Lois and I agreed they needed a good spanking.

Rwanda had blown up buildings, huts, armed tanks, battered roads and bridges, but it was absolutely beautiful with terraced hill sides. There were very few smiles like we saw in Uganda. The war had left a wall in their hearts and you could see all had in one way or the other been affected by the genocide the year before.

The orphanage broke our hearts. The children had sticks for artificial legs, some bore machete scars on their little bodies. These children had no one left in the world.

As I looked over the sea of 600 faces ages one through twenty, I cried out to God, *"Lord, how can I tell them you are a God of love."* His voice spoke almost audibly, *"Just tell them about me and my spirit will reveal who I am."* Here's where my living sacrifice *"kicked in"* I was to die to my emotions and just obey what the Lord told me to do. **"Not by might nor by power but by my Spirit, saith the Lord."** How true His Word is. I grabbed an interpreter and began to tell them who God is. Hundreds of children gathered to hear. One little girl about six years old with a torn sweater crowded near me. She did not smile. She did not talk. She would just get close to me. She carried my things as I moved to give the children room to sit down. I presented what God is. How marvelous to see the Holy Spirit quicken their little hearts. When I told them that after Jesus was crucified He was buried, in my own heart I felt I had brought out painful memories for the children. I went on to tell them, three days later, some women went to the tomb and found nothing there, and an angel told them He is risen. I couldn't finish the scripture due to the shouting of the children. They were joyful. *"Oh God, renew in me that same joy of my salvation."* Hundreds came to Christ that day. My little six-year old girl continued following me around, carrying my things, never saying a word.

After a very long day we dragged ourselves into the van and I started looking for the little girl to say good-bye. She was no where to be found. As we drove away I asked the Lord to let me see her one more time. Praise Him! She burst through the legs of the children and began running after the van as fast as she could. I signed to her *"Jesus loves you, and I love you."* After she could run no more she stopped and waved good-bye and on her precious little face I saw an ever so slight smile.

I moaned in my spirit, my eyes were full of tears. *Lord, if it is your will I will come back, and Father, give that precious 'no-name child' a hug every day for me."*

I realized each day we served in Uganda, Rwanda and also Kenya that God was calling me to serve Him and minister to the children.

Because of that calling, and because of the hundreds upon hundreds of souls that came to Christ, Satan did all he could to discourage us, cause us fear and take our lives.

One such instance came when we were going to take a boat (really a canoe) on Lake Victoria to travel to an Island where there were seven believers. After an hour into the lake a storm started washing waves into our boat. The nationals were bailing the water out and we realized we could actually die right in the middle of Lake Victoria. We call out to the Lord, and just like in the New Testament account the Lord calmed the seas and we arrived safely. Half of the Island came to the Lord including their witch doctor. He asked this question after hearing the gospel, *"I have many wives and many gods. Can I have Jesus as my Savior only?*

The Lord has done great and mighty things while the twelve of us served Him in Africa. We worked in unison letting this mind be in us which is Christ Jesus's mind.

I will return in September 1996 as a missionary to Uganda for Child Evangelism Fellowship. The next journey is just another chapter of walking by faith in obedience to His call. Not that I am anything but a *"living sacrifice"*, and I am being transformed. Praise His glorious name for His children in Uganda.

CHAPTER SEVENTEEN

A Burden For Souls

"He that goeth forth and weepeth, bearing precious seed, shall doubtless come again with rejoicing, bringing his sheaves with him."
(Psalm 126:6)

As I awoke this morning, I lifted my heart up to my Lord seeking to know His will for the day. I had spent much time with my Sunday School lesson for several days. The more I studied the less I seemed to grasp from it. I felt the need to lay it aside for awhile, then go back to it. Oh Praise the Lord, for the Holy Spirit who helps us to understand the Word of God. Also, Who alone knows who will be there and what they need at this particular time in their life.

After breakfast, I picked up a copy of the paper "Herald of His Coming," to glance over before I took my shower. I came across a testimony about Hudson Taylor. I think I have mentioned him in my previous books. Next to my Bible, the Lord used Mr. Taylor's two books, to help me grow more than any others. The first book was, *Hudson Taylor, The Growth Of A Soul."* This book begins at the time his great-grandfather was getting married. Just before the wedding was to take place he was converted and lived solely for the Lord.

As Hudson was growing up, his mother prayed much for him. One day when his mother was away from home, the Lord laid a burden for him on her heart. She went to her room and prayed until the burden lifted. Hudson was at home by himself, bored, nothing to do. He picked up a tract, and while reading it was convicted. He got down on his knees and gave his heart to the Lord.

The second book that moved me was called, *"Hudson Taylor, The Groweth Of A Work Of God."* The Lord used him to form the China Inland Mission. These two books were large volumes and it took me six months to read them. Today they are condensed into one small volume. However it is still worth reading.

I was delighted to read the testimony that he had written years ago, in this paper. I will copy quotes from it from time to time.

Just before Hudson Taylor was to leave for China, he was given a patient who had senile gangrene. The disease commenced as usual, insidiously. The patient had little idea that he was a doomed man. While he lived with Christians he was an avowed atheist. When anyone tried to talk to him about the Lord, he was very antagonistic. At one time he ordered a Scripture reader from the room with a great passion. On another occasion he spit in the face of one wanting to speak to him. Hudson Taylor became most concerned for his soul. For the first few days Hudson didn't say anything, but was praying much. By special care he was able to reduce the pain considerably to lessen his sufferings and he soon began to manifest grateful appreciation for Hudson's services.

One day with a trembling heart Hudson took advantage of his warm acknowledgments and explained it was the Lord that gave him the knowledge and power to help him. He also explained to the man that he needed to give his heart to the Lord. The man turned his back on him and while he didn't say anything, it took everything within him to keep his mouth shut. Hudson couldn't get the man out of his mind, praying constantly that the Lord would open his heart to the Word. Each day after that after he dressed the wound he would talk to him about his need. Always he would have the same reaction. He had spoken so much to the man without result. One day the thought came to him that he may be doing more harm than good causing the man to harden his heart.

That day after washing his hands he went to the door to leave, I will now quote from his word the rest, *"One day, after dressing his limb and washing my hands, instead of* returning to the bedside to speak to him, I went to the door, and stood hesitating for a few moments with the thought in mind, 'Ephraim is joined to his idols; let him alone.' I looked at the man and saw surprise, as it was the first time since speaking to him that I had attempted to leave without going up to his bedside to say a few words for my Master. I could bear it no longer. Bursting into tears, I crossed the room and said, 'My friend, whether you will hear or whether you will forbear, I must deliver my soul,' and I went on to speak very earnestly to him, telling him with many tears how much I wished he would let me pray with him.

To my unspeakable joy he did not turn away, but replied, 'If it will be a relief to you, do.' I need scarcely say that I fell on my knees and poured out my whole soul to God on his behalf. I believe the Lord then and there wrought a change in his soul.

He was never afterwards unwilling to be spoken to and prayed with, and within a few days he definitely accepted Christ as his Savior. Oh the joy it was to me to see that dear man rejoicing in the hope of the glory of God!

He told me for forty years he had never darkened the door of a church or chapel and that then—forty years ago—he had only entered a place of worship to be married, and could not be persuaded to go inside when his wife was buried."

After Hudson Taylor went to China and would be faced with things and people that there seemed no hope for, he would think of that man and how the Lord answered his prayers and would be encouraged to keep on keeping on. He often thought of the precious verse, **"He that goeth forth weeping, bearing precious seed shall doubtless come again rejoicing, bringing his sheaves with him."** We seem to have lost the gift of tears. That was what made the difference. The man saw he really cared.

We have to realize that we are all different and will have our own unique way of witnessing. I would not be comfortable following someone else, whose ways were unlike mine. Also there are many people that I may be able to reach that the other fellow couldn't touch. The ones that would respond to him would not be at all convicted by the ways that I would use. We each have to go to the Holy Spirit and seek what ways we are to approach someone because all are different.

In my earlier days, I lived with houses all around us. It was my practice to get the children off to school, do my work that had to be done, and start walking and start knocking on doors. I would see by the surroundings what they were interested in. After introducing myself we would talk about things for a period of time. One lady that I led to the Lord was concerned about her little boy's learning. Within the radius of one mile I had three children's classes. One day one of the mothers asked me why I couldn't start a group for them, through that class I was able not only to reach the mothers but quite a few attended and accepted the Lord.

To this day I still have older people ask, *"Don't you remember me? I was in your children's class."* They looked so different as they were children then. How many went on to follow the Lord, I don't know. I did what the Lord asked me to do. I sowed the seed. Only God can give the increase. As we teach we reach some through our Sunday school classes. Some people require friendship for years, and then one day a need would come into their lives and they would come to me with an open heart, and I was able to lead them to the Lord. Just being a friend, being willing to listen to the problems means a lot. I realized that in talking it out they would see the answer for themselves.

The Lord has permitted me to be an instrument in leading some of His children to a deeper walk with our Lord. Nothing planned, only a sincere desire to be used of the Lord.

I remember at one stage in my life I felt I was at a standstill. I opened my Bible and the Lord gave me a verse to show me He still had use for me. He said, *"The righteous shall flourish like the palm in the courts of our God. <u>They shall still bring forth fruit in old age;</u> they shall be fat and flourishing; to show that the Lord is upright: He is my rock, and* *there is no unrighteousness in Him."* **Psalm 92:12-15** The fourteenth verse is what spoke to me so clearly. He is letting me bear fruit through the books He has led me to write and through prayer.

We need to be available to Him, we are never too old to be used of God if we will let Him use us. He is wonderful! There is no greater joy than leading a soul to our Lord. My prayer is that He will use me as long as He chooses to leave me on this earth.

CHAPTER EIGHTEEN

God Loves A Cheerful Giver; If We Give, He Will Give

"But this I say, He which soweth sparingly shall reap also sparingly, and he that soweth bountifully shall reap also bountifully. Every man according as he purposeth in his heart, so let him give; not grudgingly, or of necessity: for God loveth a cheerful giver."
(II Corinthians 9:6-7)

The Lord brought this chapter about in a strange way. One day I was listening to the radio and the sermon was in the book of James. The subject was very interesting, and one that we need to study from time to time. The following day I picked up a study book by George Sweeting that had been given to me when I went to one of his writer's conferences. His book was also on James. As I began reading it, I thought, where have I just heard this? Then I remembered the radio program. One thing that impressed me was the teaching on the tongue. While reading it I realized that the Lord was drawing to my mind how I needed to watch my tongue. I began to talk to the Lord about it. I never try to overlook anything that the Lord brings to my attention. The next day the radio preacher said, *"You think Christians don't gossip? What about your prayer request? Do you have to give all the details? Couldn't you just ask for prayer?"*

It made me realize how much I had learned about peoples lives in that way. I had been just as guilty, as the rest, not realizing what harm I had done to people. We also gossip when we pick up the phone. The preacher suggested that we copy Psalm 141:3, *"Set a watch, Oh Lord, before my mouth; keep the door of my lips."* I am making a copy of that and will put it on my desk by the phone. I will also try to remember to lift my heart up to the Lord before picking up the phone.

Now that the Lord got across that point to me, He spoke to me about something He wants me to step out in faith to do for Him. When it is completed, I will write and tell the results of the project. Then He gave the message for this chapter. As I continued reading the book of James I began to read about giving versus not giving. It spoke to my heart. Through the years the Lord has shown me so much about this subject. He has done quite a bit in my life pertaining to giving. For example, the call to publish books, looking only to Him for the supply of the means to accomplish it. So many times He has raced to my rescue when I had no one to look to but Him. As we walk with Him, and as our love increases we want to give more, that others may come to know our precious Savior.

In Dr. Sweeting's book a testimony was given. *"Henry Crowell, founder of the Quaker Oats company was a man that knew how to use his money. When he was a young man he accepted Jesus Christ as his Savior. His business career began in a little Ohio factory, he promised God that he would honor Him in his giving. God's blessing was upon him as his business grew, he increased his giving. After a decade of faithful stewardship he testified, 'For over forty years I have given 60%-70% of my income to God. But I've never gotten ahead of God, He has always been ahead of me.'"* I too have felt many times that the Lord must have slipped into the bank and put an extra 0 on my account. It isn't something you can explain. It is just there.

What we give to our Lord is often a testimony as to how much we love Him. The story is told of a man who was asked by the I.R.S. to report to his local office. When questioned about the large sums he reported as contribution, the man produced his canceled checks as proof of his giving. The agent reviewed the checks and when he was finally convinced that the man actually did give all that money he claimed to have given, he looked at him and said, *"Sir, you certainly take your faith seriously."* That man's heart is in the right place.

There is no greater joy than to share what our Lord has so freely given us with others. Our time and our money. *"And this they did, not as we hoped, but first gave their own selves to the Lord, and unto us by the will of God."*

∧∧∧∧∧∧∧∧

"He that hasteth to be rich hath an evil eye, and considereth not that poverty shall come upon him." **Proverbs 28:22**

One day, seven financial giants met at a hotel to have a meeting. Their combined wealth totaled more than the worth of the United States treasury. People looked up to them and admired and respected them as examples of success and prosperity. But twenty-five years later a check was made on these men. Charles Schwab, president of the largest steel company, had died penniless. Arthur Cutten, a millionaire, had met the same disappointing end. Richard Witney, president of the New York Stock Exchange, had spent several years in prison. Albert Fall, a member of the presidential cabinet had been pardoned from prison so he could die at home. Jessie Livermore, the greatest *"bear"* on Wall Street, had committed suicide. Leon Fraser, the president of the bank of International Settlement, had committed suicide. Ivan Krueger, head of the world's greatest monopoly, also had taken his own life. With all their wealth and power, these men had not found happiness or lasting peace. Money can be a great blessing, but it can also be a terrible curse.

There is nothing wrong with being wealthy. The Bible does not condemn riches. Joseph of Arimathea must have been rich to own a new tomb that he gave for the burial of our Lord. Barnabas, a leader in the early church, was a wealthy man who used his money for the Lord's work. Abraham was a man of faith and a friend of God, but he also was very rich. Solomon is described in the Bible as the wealthiest man of his day. There is no harm in possessing riches; the harm is in letting riches possess you.

Money is deceiving, for it brings a false sense of security. Paul warned Timothy that *"they that will be rich fall into temptation and snares, and to many foolish and hurtful lust, which drown men in destruction and perdition. For the love of money is the root of all evil: which while some coveted after, they have erred from the faith and pierced themselves with many sorrows."* I Timothy 6:9-10

It is wrong to hoard money. I know a man that wouldn't even purchase the things that he needed, but still kept saving his money. My son used to feel sorry for him and would take him out even paying to get his clothes cleaned so as not to be ashamed of him. He lived in a little cabin and he never cleaned it. One day someone went to check on him as they hadn't seen him for awhile. Wading through old newspapers and trash that had been accumulated they stumbled over his body. He had been dead for around three days. They found out that he had a large bank account. His son, that to our knowledge never ever visited him, was left with all that money. He was the most miserable man I have ever seen. My son would bring him over to my house to get a good meal, The last time he came I sought to talk to him about the Lord I rebuked him for some of the things he said. My husband said, *"He was our guest. You shouldn't have talked to him like that."* I told him that Christ was also my guest and I would not allow anyone to talk about my Lord like that.

After restudying the book of James and thinking about others and the experiences they have gone through, and how I personally experienced the Lord work in my life; it seems that those who honor our Lord through giving back to Him a rightful portion to be used in His work God richly blessed by reaching out through giving back to Him a rightful portion to be used in His work . God richly blesses by reaching out to others that they too may come to trust Him. He keeps givers from many extra expenses because they listen to Him. Many don't take time to find out what he would have them do. As Christians we need to be especially careful that in the desire to have *'things "* we end up having nothing for the Lord.

I heard the story of a man who had barely enough to live on. He started tithing, and he was promoted and gradually reached the top. He called his preacher and told him that he could no longer afford to tithe, what should he do? His preacher said, *"We can always pray for the Lord to take you back to the amount you can afford to tithe."*

A Tithing Testimony
by Doug Dunnevant

Several years ago my friend Rick came to my office to see me. Rick was a client, and business had brought him this particular day. April the 1st—April Fool's Day. Rick was also a close Christian brother. We both attended the same church and were active in the men's Bible study that met on Thursday nights.

After we had completed our business, Rick abruptly blurted out a question . . . *"Doug, do you tithe?"* The question irritated me almost instantly. Our church was in the middle of a stewardship drive, and I had endured an entire month's worth of sermons from Malachi, hearing more about the tithe than I ever wanted to know. I was very familiar with the concept. I had grown up in a home where my parents tithed every dime they ever earned, good times and bad, and I had tithed years ago myself. But that was before . . .before mortgage payments, two children , doctor's bills and the stress and strain that a commission business can put on a family budget. And now here was Rick, stirring up trouble by bringing up the "T" word yet again.

"No, Rick," I said firmly. *"I don't tithe."*

"Why not?" he asked, smiling as if I had just told him that I didn't believe that the earth was round.

"Not that it's any of your business," I answered, not smiling, *"I don't tithe because, unlike most people, I have a very well-planned budget that accounts for every penny, and there's not enough money there for a tithe."*

There was a grain of truth to my answer. My wife,

Pam, had just given birth to our second child, and we had both decided that it was best for our family if she stayed home with our children. That decision had put a serious squeeze on our finances. Pam's teaching position provided an excellent income and benefits, and we had given it up for the sake of what we felt was God's will for us. Now I was busy trying to make up for the loss. Times were tight. Still, God was blessing my business. My career in financial services had begun to take off.

"*Okay,*" Rick said, the smile still in place. For a minute I thought I had managed to end this uncomfortable inquiry. "*Well Doug, what amount would be a month's tithe of your income?*"

Rick, who never tires of asking personal questions, was clearly up to something. I had begun to feel somewhat like the luckless wildebeest on those nature shows that always gets mauled by the tiger no matter how fast he tries to run away. Rick, the hungry tiger, was gaining ground.

"*:My income is never the same from month to month, Rick,*" I answered.

Well, what's the average? Someone who accounts for every penny like you do surely could tell me what an average month's income is."

Trapped by my own words! I gave in and offered up a number.

"*Great*" Rick shouted as he got out his company check book and began writing. "*Here's the deal. I'm going to write a check for the amount of one month's tithe, made payable to you with a date of April 30th, thirty days from today. What you're going to do is tithe during the month of April. If the end of the month comes and you're out the money, cash this check and I'll never say another word to you about this subject again . . . no hard feelings. But, if at the end of the month you can look back and see how the hand of God provided enough increase that you're not out the money, I want you to tear up this check and give testimony about the joys of tithing at our next Bible study."*

I had turned out to be the slowest wildebeest in history. Rick had maneuvered me into a corner from which there was no escape. What could I say to a proposition like this? It was a tithing guarantee of sorts, so I threw up my hands and said, *"Fine. If you want to throw away your money, that's fine with me. You're on!"*

April is not a good month to begin tithing. As I look back on it, if Rick had stopped to think what month it was maybe he wouldn't have been so quick to make a deal. Pam and I had to attend my company's convention in Colorado, so there was an airline ticket to buy. And then there was Uncle Sam to pay on the 15th. Taxes . . . Now that was something that my parents didn't have to deal with on the same scale all those years when they were tithing. They had no idea how much I had to pay in taxes and fees and business expenses. Tithing just wasn't compatible with a business like mine.

The end of the month was just two days away and all of my fears had been validated. In fact, I was $720.00 short. It wasn't even close! Rick was out his money.

I knew what my paycheck was going to be that day as I tore open the envelope. But something was wrong. Someone had made a mistake. There was an error . . . a big error! I quickly scanned the six pages of my payroll sheets trying to find the problem, and there it was at the bottom of page five. I recognized his name, although I hadn't heard from him in years. He was a client who had moved out of state several years ago. I had sold him an annuity before he left and, out of nowhere, he had apparently decided to make an additional investment. My commission netted out $725.00.

"If at the end of the month you can look back and see how the hand of God provided . . . ." Rick's words came flooding back to me now. I took the check from my desk drawer and tore it in two.

That was six years ago. I've never looked back, and God has continued to richly bless my family. For me there are so many lessons that tithing teaches. First, God is under no obligation to make me rich. That April paycheck didn't give me a record month, it simply allowed me to cover my tithe and other bills that I had incurred. I believe that tithing has absolutely nothing to do with wealth or poverty. It has nothing to do with finances, budgets or your business.

Tithing is simply about being obedient and learning to trust God. There's no other area in your life where you will see more evidence of God's hand at work. How much faith do you have? Would you like to increase your faith? Then trust God with your money. How much do you really believe the promises of the Scriptures? Would you like for those promises to become real in your life? Then trust the God of the universe with your checkbook.

My church recently asked me to give this testimony at the beginning of our stewardship emphasis month. This time the church offered a *"prove the tithe"* guarantee to anyone willing to try it for one month. Our offerings for the month broke all previous records, and the church didn't have to write anyone a check.

"Bring the whole tithe into the storehouse, that there may be food in my house. Test me in this says the Lord Almighty, and see if I will not throw open the floodgates of heaven and pour out so much blessings that you will not have enough room for it." **Malachi 3:10**

CHAPTER NINETEEN

A LIFE FULLY COMMITTED TO THE LORD

"The effectual fervent prayer of a righteous man availeth much. (James 5:16b)

      Yesterday was a wonderful day, I was on Dr. Henry's prayer calendar and Betty and Emmett came to visit me. We date from way back there. From the time she was saved Betty has been an outgoing Christian. She could approach anyone and talk to them about the Lord. She is a real soul winner. Several years ago she began having trouble with her health. Her heart pounded day and night with no relief. At times it would let up a bit but now seems to be acting up again. She has had breast cancer and had surgery for that. Then she had knee surgery. Betty is having many problems with it and is using a cane as she is still having trouble with her heart. In these latter days she feels so helpless and longs to have her strength renewed as she feels that it holds her back from serving the Lord like she wants to.
      Our Heavenly Father is wise, He doesn't let us see all the work He can do through us when we are weak. He says that His strength is made perfect in our weakness. When any work is done in the life of another, we are bound to know it is the Holy Spirit, as we know there is no possible way we could accomplish it. Therefore, our Lord gets all the glory. During this time, Emmett, her husband, too had gone through much sickness. I sometimes think Betty's middle name should be suffering. After watching this couple I know that only eternity will reveal the many

they have had a hand in leading to the Lord. Some to be ministers, and some longing for the mission field.

At this point in their lives, Emmett has retired from his church and is now associate pastor at a larger church. The retirement home that the Lord promised them years ago is almost ready for them to move into. They have named it the "Promised Land." Indeed the Lord did promise it to them. Most of their children attend this church. One day when Betty was sitting in church a lady came to her and said, "I want to touch the garment of the mother that raised a girl like Paula!

The church planned a meeting in an effort to join together both the old and the young in a mission group. They had a brunch and asked Betty's daughter, Linda, to take care of the music. There were 90 ladies there. Betty saw such love and grace in Linda. The people loved her. Linda grows more and more in love with her Lord every day. That is something to make a mother proud. Her son, Doug wrote the testimony on tithing. She has another son in Maryland. All of her children are walking with the Lord. Her life reveals Christ wherever she goes. Whenever the Lord lays on her heart to do something or to give money, she begins to pray and the Lord will send in the money or give her the strength to bake hot bread and deliver it. She doesn't let her health stand in the way of what she feels the Lord would have her do. When my children or grandchildren want something to come to pass, they say, ""*Call Betty and ask her to pray.*"

BETTY DUNNEVANT'S LIFE STORY

Have you ever been away from home, especially when you were a child, and at evening time, after the dinner hour and all the activities of the day had quieted down, felt a sense of sadness begin to evolve? Not just sadness even—but a yearning desire to be at a place called "home?" In our lives here on earth this emotion happens to some people more than others and in varying degrees of intensity. It is usually called a good case of "homesickness."

In the spiritual realm, our creator God has somehow put into the being of everyone that yearning or desire to know Him in an intimate way. Paul the apostle spoke of this in Acts 17 as he was preaching to a crowd in Athens: " ... *Men of Athens! I see that in every way you are very religious. For as I walked around and looked carefully at your objects of worship, I even found an altar with this inscription: TO AN UNKNOWN GOD. Now what you worship as something unknown I am going to proclaim to you. The God who made the world and everything in it is the Lord of heaven and earth and does not live in temples made with human hands. And He is not served by human hands, as if He needed anything, because He himself gives all men life and breath and everything else. From one man He made every nation of men, that they should inhabit the whole earth; and He determined the times set for them and the exact places where they should live. God did this so that men would seek Him and perhaps reach out for Him and find Him, though He is not far from each one of us. 'For in Him we live and move and have our being.' As some of your own poets have said, 'We are His offspring.'* (This is taken from the NEW INTERNATIONAL VERSION of the Bible.) I relate these verses to being "homesick" for Jehovah God even though in the beginning we are ignorant of what it really is that we are desiring to find or know.

When I was a little girl, perhaps five or six, I can

remember lying in bed at night with questions of all kinds going through my thoughts. One night in particular stands out in my memory for I had been asleep and suddenly I was awakened by the light of the moon shining in the window across the room. It made beautiful patterns on the floor as the gentle breeze began to stir the lace curtains at the window. At my age I was still sleeping in the room with my parents and I could hear their soft breathing as I lay there. Into my thoughts the questions began. Who made me? Who made my parents? Where did we come from? When we die where will we go? If Mama and Papa die before me, what will happen to me? Who put that beautiful moon up there in the sky? In my little girl's heart I cried out, *"Please tell me who you are!"*

    The years passed. I remember going to Sunday School and what an experience that was, for nobody in our house went except my older brother, John, and we did not go in a car, but in a boat or canoe across the mighty James River. We then had to walk more than a mile down to a village called Norwood. We were always early, so John would leave me at the house next door to the church where the Carters lived. Their daughter, Eva, was my Sunday School teacher. She was married and lived elsewhere so she would arrive just before classes began and take me to church with her.

    My class was on the second pew from the front in the church sanctuary, and the pew was always running over with squirming boys and girls. I don't remember much of anything she said about God, but my memory reveals the peace I felt each Sunday sitting on the black, shiny pew and gazing around me at the beautiful carpet, the flowers on the table at the front and, best of all, the lovely stained glass windows with various Bible characters on them. I also remember how pretty Miss Eva was and how her eyes were always sparkling as she smiled at us. I could sense how much she cared for us.

    When I was ten years old I could read well and one day some relatives came to visit since it was that time of year known as "hunting season." It was always in the fall of the year, and as we lived on a big farm, everyone would come to hunt the wild turkeys, rabbits, deer and squirrels that were abundant.

One of the men who came we called cousin Phillip, and he challenged me one day to learn the twenty-third Psalm while he was away on that day's hunt. He told me he would give me fifty cents when he got back if I knew it perfectly. Mama had to hunt up the only Bible in the house and it was the first one I had ever seen at home. Cousin Phillip found the place for me and I went out in the yard under a tree. Never will I forget that afternoon, for cousin Phillip had brought the children a bag of candy from the big city of Richmond and in that bag were pieces of taffy and lollipops. He gave me a chocolate "BB bat" and as I learned that Psalm, I would repeat a phrase and lick my chocolate. I was not so much entranced by the words as I was at the thought of having fifty cents all my own! But, as the Bible says, **"His Word will not return unto Him void,"** and as I studied, the words became sweeter than the candy and I began to read other psalms. I decided that I would read them every night before I went to bed. I don't really remember how I got the small Bible of my own. It might have belonged to my brother Lloyd who died when I was five or six years old. He had insisted on going to Sunday School as much as he was physically able and had received a Bible from that church, so probably the small one I read from each night belonged to him.

More years passed and the summer I was twelve or thirteen we went to the annual Homecoming Day services at Papa's church, Bagby Memorial Baptist Church. Mama cooked all day on Saturday getting all this lovely food ready for the biggest social gathering of the year. This usually was the beginning of a week of nightly meetings called the summer revival, and it was the only time during the year that I can remember my family going to church together.

Several things made an impression on me that day. One confusing thing was that during the dinner hour some of the "city folks" who had come from Richmond or Lynchburg in their fine, up-to-date clothes would stay together and spread their lunches on the tables made of wood that had been placed under the shade trees, while the country folk in plain but clean clothes put their meals on the back of the big work trucks they used during the week, hauling timber. To me it didn't seem quite right that there were two different groups of folks in that church and it didn't seem to me, a young girl, that they were having very much fun together.

During the afternoon there was another preaching service. In the church building the women and children usually sat on the right side and the men on the left and early before the people started to assemble for the service, my Mama would take me by the hand and we would go and sit down very quietly. As I looked around I saw on the wall a large, gold-framed picture of a man with a bushy beard and stern eyes. I leaned over to Mama and said, *"Who is that man in the picture?"* She replied, *"Hush, be quiet, don't talk loudly in here. You are in God's house!"* I kept on asking for I was determined to find out who that man was! After a few more times of asking, Mama finally said, *"You have got to be quiet, honey. That man was your great grandfather. He gave the land this church is built on. Now you be quiet."* For awhile I sat there trying to sort out why giving the land for the church should be so important if everything including the land belonged to Jesus anyway. And why put that man's picture on the wall? He didn't really own anything to give, if it all belonged to God. Finally I said, *"Mama, his picture ought not to be on the wall. Jesus' picture ought to be there if this church building really belongs to Him, don't you think?* All I got from Mama was a lot of *"Hush now, you be quiet. You are in God's house!"*

The years passed. We went through World War II. I missed my sister Ruth who had married and moved away and my brothers who had gone into the army and were halfway around the world. I especially missed my brother John, as he was always there for me. During the years I learned to cook, clean house, do laundry, and enjoy all the things of nature that the Lord had placed around me—beautiful clouds, green fields of grains, lush gardens of vegetables, fruit trees of all kinds with the beauty their blossoms brought each spring and the anticipation of seeing and eating the delicious fruits they produced, wild strawberries and luscious blackberries for the picking. Even at that time in my life these beautiful things brought forth in my heart a poem of praise and gratitude to the Lord although I did not know who He was. Life was good and the war was soon over and my brothers all came home.

In October of the year I was sixteen, one evening just before our supper hour, John asked me to go to a revival meeting with him and his new wife, Mary. After some persuasion, I agreed to go. This was held at the same church where great-grandfather's picture still hung on the wall. The preacher, Omar Burnette, began to speak and I cannot remember one thing he said, but when the man who gave the invitation got up and made his talk, I found myself going down to the front. I don't remember anything he or I said, but I was seated on the front pew and the next Sunday we went down near the church to Mallory's Creek and there I was baptized. As I look back on that experience, I believe that God truly spoke to my heart in some way. In other words, He got my attention but I know that I was not born again during that service.

This all occurred during the month of October, 1946. I was a senior in high school and a few weeks earlier had met the man of my dreams at school. He had been in the navy and now that the war was over, he had returned to finish high school. Somewhere back in those years of asking questions and reading God's Word I had discovered I could talk to this one I didn't yet know very well, and I asked Him to send me a husband. I was very particular about what kind of husband he should be. *"Let him be over six feet tall, blue eyes and black hair."* That's the description of the one God sent, Emmett Dunnevant, to whom I have been married almost 48 years AND his hair is still black!

The school year passed and the wonderful months of courtship. On July 12, 1947 Emmett and I were married at Buckingham Court House at the home of Rev. Paul Watson, a Baptist minister whom I had never seen before. Those in attendance at our wedding were John and Ruth Dixon, Horace and Mildred Dunnevant, Emmett's sisters Nancy and Emma, and the minister and his wife. We were married on a Saturday at 11:00 a.m. I wore a plain, white cotton pique dress with a small white hat I had borrowed from my sister-in-law, and a string of pearls and corsage of red roses Emmett had given me. We all went to Emmett's parents home for lunch and later in the afternoon we started on a trip to the mountains to a town called Buena Vista, Virginia. And so began our journey as a family.

We lived in Farmville, Virginia, where we both worked. Soon our first two children had arrived, a son Donnie on December 13, 1948, and daughter Linda on September 11, 1950. During the years when the children were still preschoolers, Emmett and I had to go to the city of Richmond to find jobs with some kind of future. It was such a difficult time of our lives. We lost our car and then had to leave our children with their grandparents during the week in order for us to ride the bus to Richmond and work. We would take the bus from Richmond to Farmville each Friday night and as I would sit staring into the starry sky, in my heart I was crying out to God, *"Why? Why have you let his happen to us? I've never done anything to you, God, and I love those children so much. It breaks my heart to leave them. Why have you done this to me?"*

Finally in December of that year we found a little rental house on Hopkins Road in Chesterfield county. I was sick at the time and had to quit my job, so I was home with my two children at last. Across the street from us lived a couple, Alex and Elsie Taylor. They were such good neighbors. He was a deacon at nearby Kingsland Baptist Church and they were both actively serving the Lord there. Of course, that didn't really mean anything to me at the time, but something happened a few weeks after we moved there that had a far reaching effect on my life and that of my entire family.

One day Elsie came over and asked me if I would let the children go to a Christmas party at her church. Donnie must have been about four and Linda around two. I told her I would think about it, but I really had no intention of letting them go, as I had no interest in what went on at the church. I was miserable, bemoaning the hard times that we were going through and blaming God for them. At that time in our lives the relationship between Emmett and me was strained to say the least. He worked long hours and was away almost every night working a sales job. The children were my whole life during this time as I sorted through the problems. Were Emmett and I ever going to be close again? What had happened to that life of happiness and joy I had once experienced?

The day after the party, Elsie came over to our house again and in her hands she carried two little boxes loaded with fruit, candy, and other things children would enjoy. As she came in she said, *"Well, you didn't let them go to the party, but I didn't forget them,"* and she gave Donnie and Linda the special gifts. After she left I sat there dumbfounded. *"What kind of woman was this Elsie Why should she think about my children whom she hardly knew? What kind of folks went to that church? They were certainly not like any church people I had ever known.* It was then that I decided to go to that church and see for myself what was so different about it.

The next week I asked Elsie if the children and I could ride to church with her family. She looked at me rather strangely and then said, *Why , of course you can, but you'll have to go to Sunday School, too, for we always go to that first!"* I often have thought about how much courage it must have taken Elsie to risk the fact that I would have refused to go to Sunday School too!

The next Sunday I dressed the children neatly, left Emmett asleep, and off we went with the neighbors. I was taken to a Sunday School class taught by Ruby Lee Murray and I liked her very much. Something in my heart began to warm as she taught, even though I cannot remember her words. The next Sunday we went again, and on the third Sunday, Emmett asked, *"Where are you going?"* I told him we were going to Sunday School and church with Elsie and Alex. *"Well,"* He replied, *if you had asked me, I would have taken you."* So, I asked him to join us and so began a new time in our lives, for almost every Sunday we found ourselves at Sunday School and church at Kingsland Baptist Church.

I enjoyed Ruby Lee's class so much. The people were friendly and seemed to enjoy each other's company in fellowship before class began and included everyone in their joy. One Sunday Ruby Lee asked me to stay after class and said something that surprised me very much! She told me that she was going to have to be away from Sunday School the week of Easter and the Lord had told her to ask me to teach the class for her. If she had asked me to fly to the moon and back, I would not have been more shocked! My knees began to shake at the very thought of talking in front of all those ladies. As I tried to explain my fears to her, she only replied that she knew I could do it because the Lord had told her to ask me and she knew I was the one. She also asked me to pray about it and let her know.

All that week I could not get away from her request. The more I tried to put it from my mind, the more it would surface. The thing that encouraged me to say "yes," was the thought that Ruby Lee had the confidence in me that I could do it. Here was someone who believed in me and even though I did not know it then because I was not saved, that unconditional acceptance was something my heart had been crying out for all my life. One day it would all be met in Jesus Christ.

I don't remember anything I said that day as substitute teacher. I do remember the excitement and joy I felt when the teaching time was given to me. That same excitement is present even today on every Lord's day as He gives me the privilege of sharing His wonderful Word with my class. He really is the Great Teacher!

I found out later that the trip Ruby Lee made that Easter week was to be the beginning of a much longer journey, for we learned that she had cancer and sometime later went to be with the Lord. One of our sons, Douglas, has her name Lee as his middle name because of the thanksgiving in my heart for the memory of that precious and godly lady.

Sometime during that year the church scheduled a series of nightly revival meetings. Kingsland was without a regular pastor at the time. Rev. Frank Hughes came to be the guest speaker and during that week Emmett and I went forward in the invitation time to transfer our membership to Kingsland.

Later in the year, our church called Rev. James "Jimmy" Russ as our pastor. He and his wife, Louise, had two young children. Thus began another chapter in the journey "home" for me, for the Lord was surely leading me along new paths that would one day bring me to His way and the destination of Jesus. We travel so many roads on our life's journey, but if we will let Him lead us down the roads, at every crossroads or stop sign we will hear Him say, *"This is the way, walk ye in it."*

Brother Jimmy and his family were such a blessing and joy to our church family. We knew right away that they loved us. They visited us and invited us into their home. When the youth department began to grow, they turned the basement of their house into the youth department. They sang beautiful duets together during the worship services and, best of all for me, Brother Jimmy was so careful to tell us from the Bible *"Thus saith the Lord."* When he first began to preach on Sundays he would ask, *"How many of you brought your Bibles today? Let's see. Hold them up!"* Not many had brought them and he would say, *"Listen, I want you to follow me as I read the Word so you will know for yourself that it's not just something I am telling you, so let's see how many Bibles we can have here next Sunday!"*

Five years went by and each week I sat and heard God's Word explained in such a simple way. I began to teach in the preschool class and then I moved into the children's department. In those years we had moved to nearby Colonial Heights but we still came each week to Kingsland Church. A second daughter, Paula, had joined our family by this time and, later, a son, Douglas. Louise and Jimmy had acquired some additions to their household as well since her brother's three children had come to share their home along with their new son, Randy. As you can see, the preschool department of our church was healthy and alive!

For me this was the first opportunity in my entire life that I had really heard the Bible preached and taught. As Brother Jimmy preached and he and Louise sang the wonderful, old songs of the faith, my heart was stirred. I became active in many areas of the church program. I used to wonder why it was that I never liked to teach the salvation story during those years of working with children. I discovered later that it is impossible to teach what you don't know yourself!

Time kept racing on, but God's Word was still being spoken by His faithful servant. I began to be uncomfortable during the preaching services and every time Brother Jimmy asked for those who wanted to publicly declare their decision to trust Jesus Christ as Savior, I felt inside a great desire to do something, but I truly did not know what I was supposed to do! At home I was reading my Bible and every day I listened to many preachers all day on a Christian radio station. Some of these radio evangelists were Oliver Greene, Jesse Henley, Harold Sightler, and Theodore Epp. I did not realize at the time but the Lord was using His precious Word through all of these godly men because the only way we have to become children of God is by hearing the Word. As the Bible says, **"Faith comes by hearing and hearing by the Word of God."** **Romans 10:17**

One beautiful spring morning I was outside hanging the laundry on the clothesline, thinking how beautiful the sky and clouds were. As I looked up, suddenly my heart heard these words. *"If you died today, where would you go?"* No bells began to ring, no thunder or lightning appeared, but those words were loud and clear to me. I spoke aloud, *"Why, I'm doing the best can. I hope I would go to heaven!"* Then the tears began to flow and as I entered the back door into the kitchen, I could hardly see for I could not stop crying. As I sat down, I realized that Harold Sightler was preaching on the radio, so I began to listen to what he was saying. He was telling the story from II Samuel 12 about the prophet Nathan whom God had sent on confront David about his sin. The story was about a rich man who had plenty and a poor man who only had one ewe lamb that was the family pet. The rich man took this only lamb from him. Nathan asked David, **What should be done to the rich man for this?"** David's reply was **"As the Lord liveth, the man who has done this thing shall surely die . . . "** Then, the old prophet said, **"David, you're the man,"** and he went on to relate how David had taken the wife of Uriah for himself and had Uriah killed to cover his sin. At this point in the sermon, Rev. Sightler stopped and said, *"Folks, there are a whole lot of you who are listening to me right now and you need to see that you're the man, you're the woman. I have a feeling that I'm speaking someone right now like that. Why, you might even be a Sunday School teacher, but you are still the man or woman because you have never bowed your heart or your knees to the One who can set you free and forgive you of all your sins, even Jesus."*

    I don't remember anything else he said, for at that point some of the verses of Scripture that Brother Jimmy used in his sermons began to come to my mind—almost like a recording over and over they came. **Romans 10:9-13** was the first passage: *That if thou shalt confess with thy mouth the Lord Jesus, and shalt believe in thine heart that God hath raised Him from the dead, thou shalt be saved. For with the heart man believeth unto righteousness and with the mouth confession is made unto salvation. For the Scripture saith, Whosoever believeth on Him shall not be ashamed. For there is no difference between the Jew and Greek, for the same Lord over all is rich unto all that call upon Him. For whosoever shall call upon the name of the Lord shall be saved."* When I thought through the words, *believe in your heart,"* and *confess with your mouth,"* it became as clear as day. I had never asked Jesus to forgive me for my sins! I had gone through the motions of walking a church aisle and even taught Sunday School, but the missing link was a word I had never heard and even at this point did not completely realize was the work of repentance. When we, through His grace and mercy, see ourselves as He sees and knows us and if we are willing to agree with Him that we are just like He says we are, sinners without hope, then He extends to us that beautiful invitation, ***Come unto me and live."*** In a moment that day, my sins of the past, present and future were put under the blood of Jesus Christ and a new spiritual birth experience was transacted. I still can recall the joy of that day nearly thirty-seven years ago. Even to write of it brings back the joy and although no bells tolled nor stars exploded, it seemed to me that a great, huge rock that had burdened my shoulders suddenly lifted up and to this day has never returned. I have disappointed Him so many times, but He has never disappointed me. Many times I have doubted His ways with me and others, but His wisdom has always been proven by time to be the wisest course.

The first few weeks of being a new person in Christ was a wonderful time. One of the first things I noticed was the fact that when I went to bed each night, I did not lie there and worry about the house burning down or the children getting sick or a lot of other things that probably never would happen. Also, my attitude toward my husband changed. It wasn't so much what I wanted him to do for me, but now I found myself thinking of ways to please him, even starting with what he would like for dinner each night. Answers to prayers came so often that I was overwhelmed by it all. God's Word became food for me every day and I was led by my dear friend Jo to begin a Scripture memorization course which I enjoyed very much.

One day I noticed that the joy wasn't as it had been. My prayer life began to suffer and at first I did not know why. I did know that every Sunday when Brother Jimmy would conclude his message, he always extended an invitation on behalf of Jesus for any who would like to publicly declare their allegiance to Him. I always felt very uncomfortable, not really knowing why. One day our Lord made it plain and another "why" in my life was answered.

I was reading in one of the New Testament books and a verse leaped off the page to me. *Many Jews believed on Him, but they refused to confess Him because they loved the praise of men more that the praise of God."* **John 12: 42-43** Those words described me, for during the invitation time at church I had been saying to myself, *"You don't have to go forward. You have already been baptized back there when you were sixteen. Why, what would Mr. Spivey say if now you admitted that even though you have been teaching his Sunday School for five years, you really were not saved at* *all?"* The words of the Bible convinced me that whatever people would think of me mattered not at all, but being obedient to Jesus would mean everything. I was so fearful, not knowing how to go about asking for baptism. Now that I understood what it meant, I desired to so much to obey the Lord in this way. I called Brother Jimmy and asked him if he would stop by our house. I told him everything that I have recorded here in these pages, not expecting him to understand and I ended what I had been confiding by saying, *I will understand if it would embarrass you to baptize me, being as I am already a member of the church, and if you don't want to do it I will understand, but I will go to a church somewhere that will, for I know this is what the Lord wants for me."* As I stopped talking and looked across the table at him, I noticed tears running down his face and he said, *Betty, I will baptize you anytime you say."*

I believe that day was in November of the year I was twenty-eight years old. Because of sickness among the children I was not baptized until February of the next year. It was a wonderful day especially since Emmett and I were both baptized that day, for He had been saved during those years also.

So many years have come and gone since that day at Kingsland Baptist Church. Emmett and I with our four children went out from that church to follow Jesus in the Way. He has kept every promise He ever made to us. The years seem such a little while to serve Him. So often I've not let Him use me as He wanted, but as I reflect on the past, these things from His Word I have learned:

"No good thing will He withhold from him who walks uprightly." **Psalm 84:11**
"Weeping may endure for a night but joy cometh in the morning." **Psalm 30:5**
"Now unto Him who is able to keep you from falling and present you faultless before the presence of His glory with exceeding joy, to the only wise God, our Savior, be glory and majesty, dominion and power, both now and ever. Amen." **Jude 24, 25**

CHAPTER TWENTY

THE LORD IS NO MAN'S DEBTOR

"Cast thy bread upon the waters: for thou shalt find it after many days."
                            (Ecclesiastes 11:1)

      Every so often the Lord lifts the veil and gives us a glimpse of how He is working behind the scenes. I am sure if we saw the whole picture we could not contain ourselves. All I want to do today is to offer praise to our God for the wonderful things He plans for His children.

      I have mentioned my daughter, son-in-law, and granddaughter many times in the books I have written. Now I am writing the climax as it is seen at this time. Elaine, her mother, and father, lived in a small four-room house with one bath, a small enclosed back porch, and a small front porch. The Lord began to speak to me about going to live with them (at the time that is the impression we had. My son-in-law, Norbert, felt they should look for a larger house, as we would be rather crowded in the present home. His rent at the time was $275.00 a month. As he would be walking each morning he noticed a rather large house back in the woods. It seemed abandoned. One day he stopped at the farm next to the property and asked the man about it. It seemed that his son was building it and his work ran out in that section so he would have to move away. Norbert asked the man if he thought his son would be interested in renting the property. As the house wasn't completed they said he could have it for the payments he was making on it. Which was $300.00 a month, later they increased it to $350.00.

The place was 92 feet long by 36 feet wide (I believe that is correct). It had a master bedroom, bath that was not completed. Three other bedrooms, two baths, a half bath in the mud room, large dining room, long hall, a living room, large kitchen with dining area and a large pantry. We had plenty of room, but the heating bills were enormous.

I had planned to sell my house and move there, but the Lord stopped the sale on my house, I prayed so earnestly that I wouldn't make a mistake. I let someone live in it and went to Alabama. I was there four months then I came back. This past year a hurricane knocked some trees on the house which did quite a bit of damage. The owner came back and did a lot of work on the place and fixed it so it was much warmer. Norbert is not as young as he used to be and it was taking a lot out of him to keep enough wood there to keep warm. They felt the Lord was telling them it was time to move.

One day Norbert was in the old neighborhood. He saw that their old house was for rent, so he went to see his friend who owned the house. They had just finished remodeling the place, and had added a bathroom, bedroom, and also had enclosed the back porch. When his friend found out that he was the one that wanted to rent it, he told him he could have it for the old price $275.00 a month.

When they lived there before, Elaine, who is an excellent driver was in two car wrecks. She not only demolished her new car, but her parent's car as well. All were between insurance. In order to protect herself she had to declare bankruptcy. She still paid all her bills. It later was revealed that the store she got her contacts from had given her the wrong ones and it threw her timing off. When they were without cars, Elaine bought a small car from the people they were renting from. The car was rusty but she drove it until recently, it just gave out. The bank financed a car for her with her parent's signature. As these people watched how she handled everything they were proud of her. An anonymous friend from the church gave her mother and daddy a car. It was beautiful. They asked the pastor not to tell who gave it, so they never knew.

They went to look at the house they were renting and

the owner turned to Elaine, and said, *"Elaine, if your mother and daddy died, what would you do? Would you move closer to your work?"* Elaine thought a while then she said, *"I think I would stay right here as it is half-way between my work and my church."* Then he told her that within three years they were going to give her the house as a gift from them. They will be moving in May. Isn't the Lord good! He knows when we need encouragement and He is always there.

In the meanwhile, my sister is planning on taking Betty on a cruise: just the two of them. Elaine had bought her daddy a ticket to Wisconsin where he had three wonderful weeks with his family. So the entire family was included in the blessing.

As I view this, I see God working through all that's happened. He moved them away long enough for the people to rent the other house and leave it in such a mess that the owners not only remodeled it but added the needed room. I am sure the next three years the rent will be to cover the remodeling expenses. Then they are giving it to Elaine. The lives of those three have always been open so the Lord can do miracles for them, and the world can see that the Lord is real. He takes care of His own. This family has gone through much persecution and has stood firm for their Lord.

"But this I say, he that soweth sparingly shall reap also sparingly, and he that soweth bountifully shall reap also bountifully."
II Corinthians 9:6

CHAPTER TWENTY-ONE

Let's Let Our Light Shine

"I am crucified with Christ: nevertheless I live; yet not I, but Christ liveth in me: and the life I now live in the flesh I live by the faith of the Son of God, Who loved me, and gave Himself for me." (Galatians 2:20)

As I bring this book to a close, there is so much that needs to be said. I have gained much in writing it. The many ways that our Lord has worked in the lives of others has blessed me as I read them. I can see the growth in their lives from day to day. No one stands stationary, we are either going forward or backward. May the Holy Spirit always draw us closer to our Savior.

I received a letter from Joyce Powell. As I quote this letter you will see how much she has grown in the Lord. Joyce says, and I quote, *"Praise the Lord, I sure have been crucified with Christ, and He is yet doing a great work in me. It is Christ that lives in me. I know it is by faith. Our Father is opening up His Word to me. It is such a blessing for the Lord to share what He wants us to read. He will make me like fine gold. Let His will be done in my life. I don't want to be just saved from hell, but I want all of what our Lord wants in my life. He has perfected some areas in my life. Praise God bitterness is gone. I've learned to forgive and am learning to walk in love. His peace is so great. I can just rest in Him. He called me and He gave me as a gift to the body of Christ. He will take me where He wants me to go. He says that His sheep know His voice and I am His sheep. I plan to have one of the biggest yard sales* as soon as it gets warmer. This old life is going to be very simple in the days to come. I want to have to do as little as possible in house work, spend time in God's Word, prayer, intercession, and worship with Him." She signs her name Prophetess Powell.

As I read her letter the verse came to me, *"O taste and see the Lord is good."* She has tasted and she will never be the same. We need to die daily to self so that Christ can live in us. She has come to higher ground. Praise His name!

> "His lamp am I,
> to shine where He shall say;
> And lamps are not for sunny rooms,
> Nor for the light of day;
> But for the dark places of the earth,
> Where shame, wrong and crime have birth,
> Of the murky twilight gray
> Where wandering sheep have gone astray,
> Or where the lamp of faith grows dim
> And souls are groping after Him.
> And as sometimes aflame we find,
> Clear-shining, through the night
> So dark we cannot see the lamp—
> But on see the light—
> So may I shine, His love the flame,
> That men may glorify His name."
>
> Annie Johnson Flint

May we want our lives to shine for Jesus. What about you, have you really tasted to see if our Lord is good? The time is drawing near to the coming of the Lord and we must be about our Father's business.

Only One Life Twill Soon Be Past.
Only What's Done For Christ Will Last.

EVEN SO COME QUICKLY, LORD JESUS.

BIBLIOGRAPHY

Chapter Two. *The Brown Paper Bag. The Brag Bag.*
Elenor Grace Armstrong, THE OPEN DOOR MINISTRY, c/o Gospel Tabernacle, RR2 Box 17, Coudersport PA 16915-9603.

Chapter Three. *Help, Helpers, Hope.*
Jim McKinley, 2903 Weissinger Road, Louisville KY 40241.

Chapter Three. *One Million Miles.*
Dr. J. Gordon Henry, J. Gordon Henry Ministries, 2114 Arrow Court, Murfreesboro TN 37127-5903.
 A special thanks is extended to Dr. Henry and his prayer seminar. Information about scheduling a seminar in your church or community may be obtained by contacting Dr. Henry at the above address or telephone: 615-890-8384.

Chapter Eighteen.
George Sweeting, Chancellor, Moody Bible Institute 820 North LaSalle Drive, Chicago IL 60610-3284.

Chapter Twenty-One. *His Lamp Am I.*
Annie Johnson Flint, Faith, Prayer, and Tract League 2627 Elmridge Drive NW, Grand Rapids MI 49504-1390.